THE SOCIAL CONSTRUCTION OF ANOREXIA NERVOSA

INQUIRIES IN SOCIAL CONSTRUCTION

Series editors
Kenneth J. Gergen and John Shotter

Inquiries in Social Construction is designed to facilitate across disciplinary and national boundaries, a revolutionary dialogue within the social sciences and humanities. Central to this dialogue is the idea that all presumptions of the real and the good are constructed within relations among people. This dialogue gives voice to a new range of topics, including the social construction of the person, rhetoric and narrative in the construction of reality, the role of power in making meanings, postmodernist culture and thought, discursive practices, the social constitution of the mental, dialogic process, reflexivity in theory and method, and many more. The series explores the problems and prospects generated by this new relational consciousness, and its implications for science and social life.

Also in this series

Constructing the Social
edited by Theodore R. Sarbin and John I. Kitsuse

Conversational Realities
John Shotter

Power/Gender
edited by H. Lorraine Radtke and Henderikus J. Stam

After Postmodernism
edited by Herbert W. Simons and Michael Billig

The Social Self
edited by David Bakhurst and Christine Sypnowich

Re-imagining Therapy
Eero Riikonen and Gregory Smith

Social Constructionism, Discourse and Realism
edited by Ian Parker

THE SOCIAL CONSTRUCTION OF ANOREXIA NERVOSA

JULIE HEPWORTH

SAGE Publications
London · Thousand Oaks · New Delhi

SAGE Publications Ltd
6 Bonhill Street
London EC2A 4PU

SAGE Publications Inc.
2455 Teller Road
Thousand Oaks, California 91320

SAGE Publications India Pvt Ltd
32, M-Block Market
Greater Kailash - I
New Delhi 110 048

British Library Cataloguing in Publication data

A catalogue record for this book is
available from the British Library

ISBN 0 7619 5308 6
     0 7619 5309 4 (pb)

Library of Congress catalog record available

Typeset by Type Study, Scarborough, North Yorkshire
Printed in Great Britain by Redwood Books, Trowbridge,
Wiltshire

For Lawrence and Naomi, with love

Contents

Acknowledgements

In writing the acknowledgements I finally get to thank everyone who has given me so much support from the beginning of my research and writing. I thank especially Christine Griffin who has inspired and supported me throughout, and to whom I owe so much personally and intellectually. I thank the School of Psychology at the University of Birmingham, UK, for providing me with such an enjoyable and challenging academic environment in which I developed the ideas that underpin this book. I am grateful to the librarians at the University of Birmingham, and particularly the archivists for their assistance with retrieving historical medical documents from the Medical School Library and the British Museum.

I thank Ziyad Marar, who commissioned the book, Naomi Meredith and Lucy Robinson at Sage for their editorial advice. In particular I gratefully acknowledge the support and intellectual contribution of Kenneth J. Gergen in the development of the book. More recently, thanks to Sue Widdicombe for comments.

Numerous friends, family members and colleagues provided me with continuous support and enthusiasm for the research and writing of the book. I thank all of you for that. I am especially grateful to Gary J. Krug, my partner, for many discussions, for his intellectual contributions, and the space to write when there was always so much else to do. I also thank Peter Hepworth, my grandmother, Alice, and Madeleine Murtagh for their support. Special thanks to Lawrence and Naomi who provide me with inspiration always, and have supported my writing this book in any way they could.

I am grateful to the United Kingdom Economic and Social Research Council who provided funding support during the initial stages of the research. More importantly, I thank Anthony Worsley and acknowledge the institutional support of the University of Adelaide while writing the manuscript. Thanks to Anthea Page for assisting with the initial manuscript layout.

I would also like to thank the interview participants, the health care workers, who despite having many clinical demands on their time also found the time to talk at length with me.

Chapter 2 has been published previously as 'The discovery of anorexia nervosa: discourses of the late 19th century', in *Text*, 10(4), pp. 321–38 (1990). I gratefully acknowledge Christine Griffin, who co-authored this paper with me, for allowing the use of this work in the book. The work is printed with permission of Mouton de Gruyter, a Division of Walter de Gruyter GmH & Co.

Introduction

> At first it seemed strange to me how the apparent obviousness of disease and its manifestations inside the body had eluded scientific discovery for so long. How had pre-Enlightenment generations failed to see the clearly differentiated organs and tissues of the body? Or failed to link patient symptoms with the existence of localized pathological processes? Or failed to apply the most rudimentary diagnostic techniques of physical examination? My disbelief grew until it occurred to me that perhaps I was asking the wrong questions: the problem was not how something had remained hidden for so long, but how the body had become so evident in the first place.
>
> David Armstrong, *Political Anatomy of the Body* (1983: xi)

Armstrong reflects on a time when he had wondered how so many things had eluded scientific discovery for so long, and his realization that his disbelief was a product of the kinds of questions that he had been asking. By asking different questions about how the body had become so evident, Armstrong became engaged with an analysis of the construction of knowledge and the particular construction of knowledge about the body in medical science. In other words, what we see as a phenomenon and how we understand it is always based on knowledge that is imbued with a history of language use and meaning. In this book I examine the particular construction of knowledge through which anorexia nervosa emerged as a psychiatric phenomenon.

Sir William Withey Gull (1816–90) was one of an exclusive group of eminent British physicians of the late nineteenth century who is credited with the discovery of anorexia nervosa. Originally training in medicine at Guy's Hospital London, William Gull obtained his MB degree in 1841 and gained honours in Physiology, Comparative Anatomy, Medicine and Surgery. In 1842 Gull was appointed to teach Materia Medica at Guy's Hospital, and he received from the Treasurer, Mr Harrison, a small house and a hundred pounds a year. In the following year Gull was appointed Lecturer in Natural Philosophy and contributed to the care of the patients on the wards of Guy's. Gull continued to study for some years and in 1846 gained his MD degree at the University of London, and the gold medal, the highest honour in medicine which the University can confer (Acland, 1894). In 1847 he was elected Fullerian Professor of Physiology at the Royal Institution of Great Britain, in 1858 he became full Physician, and throughout the following years his career is marked by numerous achievements and prestigious appointments. Gull was appointed Lecturer in Medicine at Guy's in 1856 until 1867, a Fellow of the Royal Society in 1858, was President of the Clinical Society between 1871 and 72, a Consulting Physician to Guy's Hospital in 1871, and increasingly served on administrative bodies, such as the Senate and the General

Medical Council of the University of London. Gull's prestigious career cul-
minated in 1872 when he became Physician to Queen Victoria.

For many years between the 1850s and 1880s Gull had a particular interest in the scientific study of dysfunction of the gastric system. Examples of
Gull's papers include 'Chronic ulcer of the stomach' and 'Fatty stools from
disease of the mesenteric glands'. During the autumn of 1868 Gull delivered
'The Address in Medicine' to the members of the British Medical Association at their annual meeting at Oxford, England. During 'The Address'
Gull made the first reference to a condition marked by the severe loss of
appetite and described 'young women emaciated to the last degree through
apepsia hysterica'. In a later paper, published in the *Transactions of the
Clinical Society* (1874), Gull refers to his earlier work on the loss of appetite. Here, Gull furnishes his audience with more detailed case description,
such as:

> Miss B., aged 18, was brought to me Oct. 8, 1868, as a case of latent tubercle.
> Her friends had been advised accordingly to take her for the coming winter to
> the South of Europe. The extremely emaciated look, much greater indeed than
> occurs for the most part in tubercular cases where patients are still going about,
> impressed me at once with the probability that I should find no visceral disease.
> Pulse 50, Reps. 16. Physical examination of the chest and abdomen discovered
> nothing abnormal. All the viscera were apparently healthy. Notwithstanding
> the great emaciation and apparent weakness, there was a peculiar restlessness,
> difficult, I was informed, to control. The mother added, 'She is never tired.'
> Amenorrhoea since Christmas 1866. The clinical details of this case were in fact
> almost identical with the preceding one, even to the number of the pulse and
> respirations. (1874: 23–4)

In this paper Gull draws the conclusion that he was observing similarities
across a number of cases and that his earlier reference to 'apepsia hysterica' should be more correctly named 'anorexia nervosa'. Gull's discovery of
anorexia nervosa resulted from his identification of the consistent absence
of gastric dysfunction which he subsequently used as sufficient evidence to
attribute the loss of appetite to a morbid mental state.

The moment when Gull defined loss of appetite as anorexia nervosa in
1874 is immensely significant because prior to this time self-starvation had
been associated with several different traditions of thinking including the-
ology, anatomy and folklore. Following Gull's 1874 paper self-starvation
became widely known as anorexia nervosa, a psychomedical condition, and
for well over a hundred years regarded as the moment when anorexia
nervosa was discovered. A major consequence of this discovery was that the
course of subsequent enquiry about anorexia nervosa became confined to
medical science and particularly the developing field of nineteenth century
psychiatry. Anorexia nervosa was swiftly accepted as a psychiatric phenomenon that resulted from psychopathology. The influence of this early classification has continued through to the late twentieth century and the
categorization of anorexia nervosa within the *Diagnostic and Statistical
Manual of Mental Disorders – IV Revised (DSM-R)* (American Psychiatric
Association, 1994). (See Box I.1.)

Box I.1   *Diagnostic criteria for 307. 1 Anorexia Nervosa*

A. Refusal to maintain body weight at or above a minimally normal weight for age and height (e.g., weight loss leading to maintenance of body weight less than 85% of that expected; or failure to make expected weight gain during period of growth, leading to body weight less than 85% of that expected).

B. Intense fear of gaining weight or becoming fat, even though underweight.

C. Disturbance in the way in which one's body weight or shape is experienced, undue influence of body weight or shape on self-evaluation, or denial of the seriousness of the current low body weight.

D. In postmenarcheal females, amenorrhea, i.e. the absence of at least three consecutive menstrual cycles. (A woman is considered to have amenorrhea if her periods occur following hormone, e.g. estrogen, administration.)

Specify type:

Restricting Type: during the current episode of Anorexia Nervosa, the person has not regularly engaged in binge-eating or purging behavior (i.e., self-induced vomiting or the misuse of laxatives, diuretics, or enemas).
Binge-Eating/Purging Type: during the current episode of Anorexia Nervosa, the person has regularly engaged in binge-eating or purging behavior (i.e., self-induced vomiting or the misuse of laxatives, diuretics, or enemas).

My aim is to challenge the dominant conceptualization of anorexia nervosa as a psychopathology. In writing this book I am not concerned with arguing for the recognition that various social and cultural aspects of western societies contribute to the onset of anorexia nervosa. Rather, my central thesis is that the dominant psychiatric definition of anorexia nervosa is socially constructed through discourse or, in other words, regularly occurring systems of language. Throughout *The Social Construction of Anorexia Nervosa* I examine the ways in which different forms of knowledge emerged during specific historical periods in western societies to construct anorexia nervosa as an object of medical science. Further, I examine how explanations of anorexia nervosa accorded with the dominant ideas of science, medicine and women. I explore the interrelations that exist between these forms of knowledge, the use of language and social practices.

Discourses involve practices that position the subjects of the diagnosis of anorexia nervosa in *particular* ways and in turn reproduce dominant ideas about the phenomenon. In the case of anorexia nervosa particular discourses coalesced during the late nineteenth century to produce a set of statements and practices that later established medicine, psychiatry and psychology as having the capacity both to explain the loss of appetite in women and to intervene in specific ways to change their behaviours.

These discourses explain and justify the practices within the human science disciplines such that they appear as the taken-for-granted and 'natural' understandings of phenomena. Discourses also operate across disciplines, linking beliefs, values and expectations together, especially when they refer to social groups, such as women, gay and lesbian groups, and groups who are stigmatized because of disease. Therefore, parallel to a historical analysis of these medicalizing discourses runs an analysis of the positioning of women as subjects within the discourses of medicine, psychiatry and psychology.

My analysis of language and practices through which anorexia nervosa emerged is informed by several schools of thought in the social sciences and humanities, including poststructuralism, feminism and psychology. I will briefly introduce one of these schools that is most pertinent to my analysis under the heading, poststructuralism, and particularly the writings of the French philosopher of language Michel Foucault. I will then go on to describe the structure of the book and the different ways of reading the central thesis.

Poststructuralism and the analysis of language

Poststructuralism is a philosophical movement that draws on numerous disciplines such as linguistics, literary studies, sociology, social psychology and cultural studies to analyse the ways in which phenomena are constructed through structures of language. Structuralism considers language and the role of social structures to be the most important factors in the construction of consciousness, and the subsequent shaping of human autonomy (Sturrock, 1986). Poststructuralist theory developed from structuralism, not as an antithetical movement, but developed in relation to specific schools of socio-political thought and their analyses of the significance of language and social practices. Michel Foucault's philosophy of language is a form of poststructuralist analysis in which discourses are specific to historical and social periods and in turn become reproduced through relationships between power, knowledge and institutional authority. I draw on Foucauldian analysis to examine the construction of anorexia nervosa, by systematically analysing key historical texts about anorexia nervosa to trace how it became defined as an object of science, and the positions made available to women, and in some instances men, as subjects of that definition. My analysis builds a critical framework for reconceptualizing anorexia nervosa by documenting the ways in which language is used to explain, justify and reproduce particular social practices. The historical, social and cultural dimensions of anorexia nervosa have traditionally been regarded within the human sciences as being influences on individual behaviours and separable from subjectivity. I challenge the notion that anorexia nervosa is separable from the social practices through which it became defined and understood as a predominantly psychomedical condition.

The deconstruction of anorexia nervosa enables us to ask different questions and develop an understanding about historical, social and cultural dimensions, not as being separable entities, but involving particular social practices that constructed a dominant conceptualization of anorexia nervosa. I examine the functions that discourses have in terms of how agreements were produced about what constituted scientific knowledge within medicine, knowledge within other disciplines, and the relationship of these to the explanation of women and psychology. Further to this, I argue that the discourses of anorexia nervosa both constitute and explain contemporary health care practices and in turn reproduce long-standing approaches to clinical management. This book demonstrates the *structuring* of language and its *effects* on both disciplines and subjectivities.

Foucault and the analysis of historical concepts

The writings of French philosopher Michel Foucault, and the influences of Georges Canguilhem and Gaston Bachelard on Foucault's work, have been crucial to my analysis of the emergence of anorexia nervosa as a historical medical concept. Bachelard's philosophy of science was published in a series of works during 1927–53 in which he emphasized the importance of understanding reason through accounts of science and that these should be seen as developing historically. Canguilhem's history of science is based on what he termed 'a history of concepts'. The concept was more important to Canguilhem than the theory. Central to Canguilhem's philosophy is discussion of the notion that the same concept can be present in several and very different theories. In particular, I have drawn on Foucault's *Madness and Civilisation* (1971), *The Birth of the Clinic* (1973) and *The Archaeology of Knowledge* (1974) to elaborate my analysis of the historical significance of anorexia nervosa.

In direct contrast to the dominant view of history that events occur on a sequential and progressive basis, Foucault focuses on disjunctures, irregularities and contradictions that rejected the linear path of traditional history. Foucault's work is commonly regarded as constituting two strands of methodology; structuralist and genealogical. The structuralist position demonstrates how certain forms of knowledge were allowed and others were not during different historical periods due to their relations with institutions of power. Genealogical analysis concentrates on the historical development of concepts, and understands history as 'effective' or 'general' history.

> This emphasis within genealogy is disruptive of traditional historical analyses employing conceptions of uninterrupted continuities in history: it disturbs the formerly secure foundations of our knowledge and understanding – not, however, in order to substitute an alternative and more secure foundation, but to produce an awareness of the complexity, contingency and fragility of historical forms and events to which 'traditional' history has attributed a stability. (Smart, 1983: 76)

I trace the discovery of anorexia nervosa during the late nineteenth century and argue that it emerged through a particular configuration of social, political and ideological thinking. Three areas of analysis are of particular importance throughout the book: the rise of scientific medicine during the nineteenth century; the relationship between women and psychiatry; and how socio-political ideas, including those emanating from theories about women, society and morality, together with professional claims of scientific truth, became incorporated into organized systems of thought and employed in psychological medicine.

In *The Social Construction of Anorexia Nervosa* I have drawn on a range of critical analyses of medical science and psychiatry, and poststructuralist philosophies, to demonstrate how anorexia nervosa is a product of medical science. Medical science and psychiatry are always brought together in social and linguistic practices that construct specific objects of scientific enquiry and particular ways, or discourses, to explain those objects. William Gull's (1874) discovery of anorexia nervosa is significant because it was the moment when anorexia nervosa formally became an object of medical science. The analysis of social practices provides an account of how and why anorexia nervosa was a discovery of the late nineteenth century. This discovery was not simply a reflection of scientific truth but emerged through a set of interrelated discourses and social practices. The explanation of anorexia nervosa in 1874 as a form of psychopathology drew heavily on theories of hysteria which was the dominant discourse through which women were interpreted in relation to insanity. Over a hundred years later there are numerous explanations of anorexia nervosa; some of the key ones being biomedical, familial, socio-cultural and feminist. This number of explanations attests to the competing discourse of science.

The social construction of medicine

Foucault was most interested in the philosophy of ideas, with his early work focusing on the emergence of medicine and psychiatry. One of Foucault's key analytical frameworks, the *analysis of emergence,* informs my analysis of anorexia nervosa as a concept that is embedded in historical, social, and political discourses and practices. While Foucault's methods inform the writing of this book, it should not be assumed that Foucault is discussed as a social constructionist. Analyses of the social construction of medicine draw on a range of disciplines and constructionist theories to elucidate the historical, social, and political processes involved in securing medical ideas and practices. As Jordanova writes:

> It may be fruitful to think of social constructionism as delineating a space which the social history of medicine can occupy. By stressing the ways in which scientific and medical ideas and practices are shaped in a given context, it enjoins historians to conceptualize, explain and interpret the processes through which this happens. (1995: 362)

Since the 1970s and early 1980s many authors have explicated the social and cultural relations of language production. Some of the key writings are: Gergen (1985); Henriques et al. (1984); Parker (1989, 1992); Potter and

Wetherell (1987); and Shotter and Gergen (1989). These writings brought questions about language, discourse, and social and political practices to the fore in psychology, and an increased use of related methodologies, such as narrative and discourse analyses, for research. Some of this research, termed critical psychology, has examined psychiatric categories using deconstruction (cf. Harper, 1994; Hepworth and Griffin, 1990; and Parker et al., 1995). Critical psychologists argue that specific social and political practices during different historical periods made it possible for particular professions to emerge and define the objects of the medical gaze, such as anorexia nervosa (Hepworth and Griffin, 1990). Similarly, Harper (1994) analyses an account of the category of mental disorder 'paranoia' written by the British psychiatrist Aubrey Lewis. Lewis' account of paranoia, Harper (1994) argues, is embedded within the ideological, political and professional context of its writing that contributed to the development of the concept and its practical usage.

Writers using social constructionism have drawn on Foucault as well as many other philosophers in the analyses of the construction, use and functions of language. Social constructionism also has various critics. This body of criticism is not the subject of this book but is included to indicate to the reader that some dissent for social constructionism exists. Since the early 1980s and widespread use of social constructionism in disciplines such as sociology and psychology there has been vigorous methodological debate, within which, for example, Bury (1986) criticizes its potential utility for medical sociology. For an excellent discussion of the criticism of social constructionism see Nicolson and McLaughlin's (1987) reply to Bury.

Drawing on Foucauldian analysis enables the development of a different interpretation of anorexia nervosa as an object of medical discourse that contrasts with its long-standing status as a disease entity. This long-standing and dominant conceptualization of anorexia nervosa has led to a proliferation of aetiological explanations of anorexia nervosa that remain unsubstantiated as specific causal factors and form part of a common multidimensional model (cf. Garfinkel and Garner, 1982). The plethora of research and theory about anorexia nervosa is not owing to the resistant or complex nature of anorexia nervosa as a disease entity. The diverse range of explanatory theories, psychopathological models of anorexia nervosa, and various treatment approaches, including the multidimensional approach, has emerged in relation to the development of the human sciences during the late nineteenth and twentieth centuries. This literature reflects the concomitant processes of the human sciences, such as the diversification of discipline based knowledge, processes of normative health sciences, professionalization of health care services and the role of expert knowledge and medical dominance.

However, given the recognition that the processes of the human sciences produce certain ways of thinking about phenomena, to what extent should examination of these processes direct the debate about anorexia nervosa? It is this question that the book addresses in discussing the structural, political and institutional relations between anorexia nervosa, medical science and health care. Although, in the examination of the social construction of anorexia nervosa as a psychiatric condition it should not be assumed that generalizations could be made to other areas of mental illness classification in contemporary psychiatry. The historical emergence and specific social practices that contributed to the discovery of anorexia nervosa have implications for understanding its psychiatric classification, but this argument does not extend to other categories of mental illness as corollaries of this argument.

Book structure

Overall, the book is an account of the history of knowledge about anorexia nervosa. The book is structured into three parts and each part relates to key debates in the field of eating disorders. In Part I, I identify and critically discuss four key periods in the evolution of ideas about anorexia nervosa; religious interpretations of self-starvation, medical, socio-cultural and feminist discourses. In Chapter 1 the transition from religious to medical authority, ideas about morality and women, and the legitimization of social practices are discussed in terms of their significance to the emergence of anorexia nervosa as a medical concept. The central focus of Chapter 2 is a discourse analysis of the late nineteenth century discovery of anorexia nervosa as a psychomedical condition. I analyse the emergence of concepts that became integral to dominant ideas about anorexia nervosa, identify key discourses that were necessary to its discovery, the interrelations between discourses and the subject positions available to women. In Chapter 3 I critically examine some of the historical developments in psychological literature that moved away from the medical model towards a social perspective on mental health and the first feminist texts that aimed to challenge the medical model of anorexia nervosa. Within these key periods medical and feminist perspectives are of particular interest because of their conflicting paradigms of knowledge.

Part II is based on a series of interviews with health care workers and demonstrates various ways in which dominant ideas about anorexia nervosa are maintained and reproduced in therapeutic practice. The form of discourse analysis in these chapters focuses on language use and is informed by, for example, the work of Potter and Wetherell (1987). I analyse the ways in which arguments and reasons are proposed as justifications or structured in relation to professional identities. Chapters 4, 5 and 6 focus on constructions of gender and identity; the cause of anorexia nervosa; and clinical treatments respectively.

In Part III I discuss recent theoretical developments in postmodern and poststructuralist philosophies that have put forward reinterpretations of eating disorders. The shift from the modern to the postmodern in the explication of individual psychology, the body and social practices, is introduced by drawing on writings from feminism, postmodernism and poststructuralism, as well as those writings that specifically address anorexia nervosa. The turn to language and postmodernism within the human sciences during the twentieth century has increasingly questioned the authority of science and medical knowledge. Postmodernist ideas challenge the underlying assumption that knowledge and science are epistemologically and methodologically unified and that an ultimate truth is possible (Seidman and Wagner, 1991). Postmodern ideas about anorexia nervosa have introduced new forms of understanding the processes of therapy which have mostly come under the rubric of narrative therapy affiliated with the work of Michael White and David Epston (1989, 1990). The use of narrative therapy as a conceptual framework for both anorexia nervosa and therapeutic practices is critically examined. In the concluding chapter I outline a direction for prevention and treatment strategies in which anorexia nervosa is a public rather than an individual problem that requires a participatory approach to changing health care practices.

Reading the book

This book can be read in many ways. I have not attempted to document a continuous history of anorexia nervosa to the present, rather I analyse examples of historical medical documents on anorexia nervosa that will be of particular interest to some readers. The book documents the key moments in the emergence of the definition of the term anorexia nervosa. Further to this, there are summaries of historical developments during the late twentieth century when feminist analyses of anorexia nervosa attempted to challenge the medical model of eating disorders. I discuss some of the late twentieth century debates about the significance of the body in the human sciences and postmodern theories of the body. The recent theoretical developments are integrated with a critical examination of narrative therapy and its use in relation to anorexia nervosa. The discussion of these areas will be of interest to the general reader who is familiar with the developing explanations of anorexia nervosa, medicine and psychotherapy.

For the reader who has a modern scientific background the book will illustrate some of the key differences between modern scientific explanation and social constructionist explanations of anorexia nervosa. It is important to make clear some of the differences between these paradigms of enquiry because the majority of explanations of anorexia nervosa are discussed within the framework of modern science. My analytical approach, particularly in Chapters 2, 4, 5 and 6, is based on poststructuralism and the examination of the constructive role of language related to specific historical and social periods. Discourses privilege one way of explaining a phenomenon over another during different historical periods, and by examining discourses we understand how human actions are structured, explained, maintained, reproduced and changed. This is a very different conceptualization of knowledge from modernist scientific thought. Eating disorders research is commonly judged in relation to the criteria of the scientific method, it is, however, uncommon for medicine, psychiatry and psychology to report research evidence in terms of this specific scientific framework. In other words, the dominant concept of scientific enquiry serves the function of maintaining the long-standing tradition that there is only one interpretation of an object of enquiry, and that the truth about this object is discoverable through the application of modernist scientific methods.

Poststructuralism, as well as other philosophies of knowledge, have clearly documented a number of interpretative methods, and challenged the claims to truth of the modern human sciences. The consideration of these various research traditions, criticisms and methodologies should be more fully represented in the field of eating disorders. Instead, the field continues to be dominated by the repetition of a scientific approach that has neither provided the scientific evidence of the causation of anorexia nervosa that it has sought for over one hundred years, nor the direction for developing more effective prevention and treatment strategies.

Despite increased interest since the 1970s in the social and cultural dimensions of anorexia nervosa much of this research has been brought within a scientific hegemony and made to 'fit' the modern scientific criteria for establishing claims to truth. The problem of the social and cultural aspects of anorexia nervosa and how these are addressed within preventive and treatment practices is less to do with explanation and more to do with which knowledge and whose knowledge will be allowed into the debates. Much has already been conceived in terms of the social and cultural aspects of eating disorders through various theorizations. To readers without any prior reading of the philosophy of science this book should challenge them to reflect on how conclusions about the interpretation of anorexia nervosa in this book are made, what kinds of knowledge inform these conclusions, and the effects of the conclusions on changing practices.

For those readers who are immersed in social constructionism, discourse studies and the turn to language in psychology, this book can be read as a contribution to the field. The deconstruction of the language used to define, manage and limit the explanations of anorexia nervosa is a form of resistance to the dominance of historical psychomedical ideas and practices. It is through making visible the effects of those practices that the possibilities for changing the discourses about women and anorexia nervosa become elaborated.

For readers who are also the subjects of the diagnosis of anorexia nervosa and psychiatric practices, persons who self-starve, this book can be read as a counter-text. It is not my intention to deny that a form of distress related to eating and food exists, but that the categorization of this distress, in which anorexia nervosa is regarded as a manifestation of psychopathology, is contested. This book describes another history of how and why current therapy practices exist, how the organization of experts and patients emerged in relation to anorexia nervosa, and some of the reasons for the limitations of psychomedical as well as other interventions.

All knowledge, whether it derives from modern science or postmodern, interpretative schools of thought, is discursive. Knowledge is communicated and understood by systems of thinking, and rules of language use that are constructed through social practices. In *The Social Construction of Anorexia Nervosa* I analyse these systems of thinking and the formation of key discourses that construct contemporary practices and the limits to those practices. My main aim throughout the book is to locate possibilities for the creation of spaces to move beyond the reproduction of ineffective practices towards new ways of conceptualizing anorexia nervosa that inform prevention treatment strategies.

PART I
EARLY IDEAS ABOUT SELF-STARVATION AND ANOREXIA NERVOSA

1
From Religion to Madness: Religious and Medical Interpretations of Self-starvation

The purpose of this chapter is to introduce the interpretations of self-starvation prior to the medical discovery of anorexia nervosa in 1874. The dominant interpretations drew on religion, and with the phrase religious interpretation, I am confining the definition of religion to Western Christianity. These early interpretations are important because they provide very different explanations of the relationships between women and food, and demonstrate how interpretations of behaviours accord with the dominant ideas of particular historical periods. In order to elaborate on the religious interpretations of self-starvation I will discuss three key themes. The first theme discusses the religious interpretations of women during the twelfth and thirteenth centuries and from the seventeenth century onwards. The second theme briefly describes the emergence of the concept of madness. The third theme focuses on the transition from religious to medical authority. These themes do not stand in isolation from one another, rather, they are key sites when ideas emerged during different periods and resulted in specific practices that defined and regulated women. Finally, I draw conclusions about the significance that these ideas had for the interpretation of self-starvation and their relationship to the medical discovery of anorexia nervosa.

Self-starvation and women Saints

Women who starved themselves were undoubtedly most highly esteemed as a result of their fasting during the twelfth and thirteenth centuries where records show these women being deemed Saints. Women's fasting in early religious thought constituted a 'miracle of existence' without nourishment. There are several descriptions of women in clerical texts in which their fasting is interpreted as a form of asceticism. These writings firmly secured the relationship between asceticism, women and food, continuing, in some instances, into later centuries. One well-known example of fasting women was Catherine of Siena (1347–80) who, like some other women, was regarded as a Saint by men with religious authority. Cohn describes the diet and decline of Catherine of Siena:

> From the age of fifteen Catherine Benincasa, better known as Catherine of Siena, consumed nothing but bread, uncooked vegetables, and water; from the age of twenty-five she simply chewed on bitter herbs, spitting out the substance . . . In the end she refused even to drink water and so, in her early thirties, put an end to her life. (1986: 3)

There were several aspects of the twelfth and thirteenth century religious context which structured women's participation in this holy realm. 'Eucharist devotion' was a significant theme in the articulation of women's piety. Women practised this devotion as the devotion of those who receive rather than consecrate, and which came to them through inspiration rather than through office or worldly power (Walker Bynum, 1991). The difference between these two forms of devotion is significant because women who received were overwhelmingly passive within their relationships with clerics. Even women's participation in religious ceremonies had to be sanctioned by male clerics.

The fasting practices of women Saints closely approximate the practices involved in the self-denial of food by women diagnosed with anorexia nervosa in the late twentieth century (Bell, 1985; Walker Bynum, 1991). The relationship between women's self-denial of food and asceticism is represented as an expression of women's social and psychological conditions. Bell's (1985) conceptualization of 'holy anorexia' maintains there is a direct link between medieval women's fasting and the modern form of anorexia nervosa. For Bell the intense relationships between women and holiness and women and thinness represent ideal states of being in a struggle to assert female identity in a world dominated by men (Cohn, 1986). However, this argument relies on the notion that religious devotion appealed to women and that self-starvation became an expression of their own pursuit of salvation. Furthermore, this argument draws heavily on the idea that women had a particular propensity to express a motif of immortality. Walker Bynum's (1991) examination of twelfth and thirteenth century female Saints emphasizes the symbolic dimension of women's use of the Eucharist, locating fasting and the use of specific foods, such as meat, in a discourse of control. During the times that the woman's corporality conflicted with either the wish of her family and/or religious advisers, the only control she could execute was over her body. The times when punishment was imminent, women, unlike men, did not have external objects that they could renounce, such as property, and women's bodies became the object of revulsion and punishment.

Walker Bynum's (1991) work delineates between the psychological and social conditions that were linked to women expressing spirituality through the body. This work also informs us about how historic fasting practices formed some of the early associations between women and the body. Unlike traditional psychiatric views of self-starvation that were established during the late nineteenth century, Walker Bynum's (1991) analysis does not require an appeal to the notion of an inherent female psyche. Arguments that appeal to the female psyche in explanation of anorexia nervosa commonly describe aspects of this psyche that remain indecipherable to experts, such as the physician. This inexorable link between women, corporality and the dominant explanation of women has continued since at least the twelfth and thirteenth centuries. The discursive construction of this corporality can tell us just as much about the explanation of women during different historical periods as it can about the construction of theories and by whom.

The religious interpretation of women and fasting related to sainthood was a considerable privilege within that early period, and those women stand in stark contrast to clerics' definition of other groups of women as 'witches' during the fifteenth and sixteenth centuries. It would be simplistic to assume that the religious interpretation of women and ecclesiastical authority over women bestowed upon them a unified and positive status. Rather, there were considerable shifts in the religious interpretations of women related to who the women were and what differences they exhibited compared to the social norms of the period. Common to all groups of women was that they were always in the position of being the subjects of dominant religious ideas about their actions. Early religious ideas did not specifically interpret fasting as a form of madness; the ideas that they did hold, like subsequent dominant interpretations, always explained women as the Other. Socially and ideologically women constituted the Other, with men being the norm against which women were evaluated and their actions defined. In this sense the early theological ideas about women and femininity also defined masculinity and created a position for men to dominate the interpretation of women's actions. In later religious thought clerics assumed women possessed an inferior morality and that this was intrinsic to the female character. For these reasons clerics policed women's actions and sought evidence of immoral behaviours.

Religious beliefs developed into sophisticated sets of arguments that defined femininity in terms of good and evil, which was later to become significant in the representation of women and the construction of various dualisms, the most famous being the Madonna and Whore (Ussher, 1991). The most significant shift in the religious interpretation of women and self-starvation was away from sainthood towards women being regarded as manipulative and deceitful (cf. Ehrenreich and English, 1979). This shift in the representations and interpretations of women continued throughout the Middle Ages through to the eighteenth and nineteenth centuries. The most profound example of the effects of the religious interpretation of women as the Other, and the struggle over control, is found in the witch-hunts of the fifteenth and sixteenth centuries.

In the next section the witch-hunts are discussed in more detail and are important to the understanding of the religious interpretation of women for two main reasons. First, the religious interpretation of women varied in relation to different women and during particular historical periods. Religious authority was based on the notion of good or evil, and women who carried out practices that were different from those practices founded upon religious knowledge were deemed as being possessed by evil. This difference was enough, therefore, to define, identify and justify the attempts to eradicate a large number of women. This notion of good and evil occurred in relation to a group of women who were blatantly mounting a threat to the dominant practices of healing and had a developing form of knowledge that was not based upon religious doctrine. The religious establishment responded so vehemently to this group of women because they challenged religious orthodoxy and threatened the organization of knowledge and practices about healing in those societies at that time. Conversely, earlier religious interpretations of women who were fasting were held in high esteem as a consequence of their actions, but their fasting posed little threat to the social order and afforded those with religious authority to respond in a way that privileged women.

The second point about the significance of the witch-hunts is the way in which they relied upon early notions of good and evil and the relationship of this to the separation between reason and unreason. The religious interpretation of a group of women who were different from the prevailing social norms and dominant ideas about women as being witches preceded the organization, segregation and anihilation of that group to maintain social control. The witch-hunts are an early form of the definition of deviant groups and the resulting tactics that religious authorities employed in the name of Christianity. These processes of identification and tactics of segregation became fundamental to the organization of sane from insane populations. The separation and categorizing of behaviours was a central tenet of the distinction between sanity and madness (Foucault, 1971), and the definition of specific abnormal behaviours, such as anorexia nervosa.

Religious interpretation of women and the witch-hunts of the Middle Ages

Women comprised the main group who were persecuted during the 'witch-hunts' of the Middle Ages and made culpable for the ills of a society. The movement was given force, fervour and sanction by religious establishments. Monks and priests throughout Europe presided over the persecution of women and the resulting deaths. The witch-hunts are a spectacular example of the religious management of deviance and a precursor to later conceptualizations of women and 'deviant' behaviours. The targets of witch-hunts, while not being exclusively women, were overwhelmingly peasant women. Women were persecuted for a broad range of reasons and particularly, feminist writers have argued, for practising lay healing and midwifery skills (Ehrenreich and English, 1979). These practices were seen as '"evil deeds" and were being carried out with the help of the devil' (Parrinder, 1958: 97). Rather, the healing practices challenged the dominance, power and authority of men who controlled religious knowledge and practices that had institutional sanction. The extensive nature of this persecution indicates that these women were perceived as presenting a serious threat to the religious order.

The witch-hunts of the fifteenth and sixteenth centuries spread through Germany and Italy and led to thousands of executions. For example, 900 'witches' were executed in one year in Wurzburg (Ehrenreich and English, 1979). Executions were carried out on young and old women and children. By the mid-sixteenth century witch-hunts were common in England and France. Women were charged with copulating with the devil, rendering men impotent and then imprisoning a man's penis in a basket, devouring newborn babies and poisoning livestock (Ehrenreich and English, 1979). Witch-hunts are an example of ideology in practice and a form of social practice that was legitimated through the religious construction of femininity that included the belief that women could harbour the devil. Synnott (1993) argues that the long-standing beliefs about women as sinful and sexual pleasure as sinful provide the preconditions for the persecution of the witches in Europe and North America. This practice was much more than a short-lived phenomenon. It became an organized, large-scale system of governing women and 'deviants'. The document that dealt with witches, the *Malleus Malleficarum*, showed a greater resemblance to a legal than to a medical document with the ferreting out of witches and the proving of witchcraft as being preliminary to sentencing (Szasz, 1972).

Feminist analysis of the practice of witch-hunts argues that the officiating over witch-hunts by monks and priests and the charges they made against women are nothing more than misogynist fantasies (Ehrenreich and English, 1979). The charges against women were targeted at women's early skills of abortion and the administration of herbal remedies. However, Hasted (1984) has criticized the argument that the persecution of 'witches' during the Middle Ages was related to the challenge that women posed to clerics/physicians and patriarchal control over women's bodies. Drawing on the example of the trial of the 'Pendle Witches', named after the area of Lancashire, England, Hasted argues that the skills of these women did not pose such a great threat to male physicians of the time because they were quite different forms of enquiry and practice. Therefore, the idea of the 'witch' as a persecuted lay healer does 'not provide a blanket explanation for the motives of the prosecutions in every case' (1984: 17). Rather, the witch-hunts, in some cases may have been attributable to women holding a more generalized view of life that was regarded as unacceptable for women at the time (Hasted, 1984).

Common to many analyses of witch-hunts is the notion that they performed an early function of identifying social groups that deviated from the norms of the male-dominated religious establishment and their segregation or anihilation contributed to re-establishing social order. Clerics presided over societal morality and had a monopoly over the early management of the female body. Christian ministers advised young women on the attributes of a useful life-style (Turner, 1982). During times of social upheaval women became the scapegoats in the resolution of socio-political problems. The practice of using particular social groups for the purpose of scapegoating is common throughout history. For example, woodcuts from the fifteenth century depict the burning of Jews as scapegoats for the plague (cf. Lyons and Petrucelli, 1978). Scapegoating developed as a social process whereby the Otherness in our lives is defined through the demarcation of boundaries between social groups (Foucault, 1971). It is not the case that these groups already existed *waiting* to become scapegoats, but that dominant ideologies constructed specific groups as having significant and culpable associations with various aspects of Otherness.

The key link between the period in which women were persecuted as witches and later interpretations of self-starvation and the medical construction of female madness is formed through the notion of hysteria. Hysteria, originating from the Greek word *hysteria*, meaning womb, was thought to be the cause of witchcraft. Hysteria became a metaphor for the explanation of women across many situations, not only in the persecution of witches, but women in general. Hysteria constituted a major attack on women that was aimed at that which was most specific to women and symbolic of feminine power: the womb. Increasingly, throughout the sixteenth and seventeenth centuries and the early transition from religious to medical authority over the interpretation of women, hysteria became identified as the cause of nervous diseases in women.

The emergence of madness during the eighteenth century

There are numerous writings that document histories of madness, insanity and psychiatry, one of the most well known being Michel Foucault's work on the emergence of madness. Foucault's conceptualization of historical analysis, often depicted by the notion of the 'history of the present', provides the possibilities for further interpreting the emergence of madness and explaining how the very artefacts of this emergence reproduce the conditions for contemporary practices. This history of madness, the analytic form of Foucault's work, is a theme that is continued throughout the book and constitutes an important difference in developing alternative conceptualizations of self-starvation, the discovery of anorexia nervosa, and the explanation of contemporary practices as being constitutive of this history.

The emergence of new discourses of power out of Enlightenment philosophies gradually displaced the religious discourses in both language and practice, often creating new settings in which the new powers could be exercised. Foucault (1971) argued that the segregation of groups with leprosy during the Middle Ages and housed in leprosariums across Europe had particular significance for the emerging notion of insanity. Lepers were confined to these special institutions and stigmatized because of the meanings that leprosy represented, such as uncleanliness and fears of contagion. The segregation of infected persons and confinement within purpose built buildings was an early form of 'dividing practices' that later extended to other groups and was functional in regulating social order (Foucault, 1971). These early practices that aimed to regulate those infected with leprosy were crucial to representations of insanity and in formulating understandings of the 'insane'. The social structures which excluded populations from society returned in the seventeenth and eighteenth centuries when the poor, criminals and the 'deranged' were compelled to live in institutions vacated by lepers. This movement associated madness with the legacy of leprosy – contagion and disease – and became influential in the medicalization of madness (Foucault, 1971).

The separation of reason from unreason began during the Middle Ages. Before the seventeenth century unreason had been defined as having some creative and instructive value, but during the seventeenth century the meaning of reason changed, and madness was seen as false reason (Foucault, 1971). A key moment in the history of madness was the opening of the *Hôspital Général* in 1656, which worked towards the prevention of mendicancy and idleness, thought to be the source of disorders (Foucault, 1971). The period during the seventeenth and eighteenth centuries is referred to by Foucault as the Great Confinement, and he states that up to as late as 1815 in Paris and London it was common practice to display the 'insane'. 'Lunatics' were chained to walls and beds, women had feet and fists bound and were kept in pigsties, whilst onlookers paid one penny at Bethlem, London, to wonder at them (Foucault, 1971). Images which depicted the animality of madness ruled this period. Madness became a spectacle because the 'insane' were seen as being unable to suppress the bestiality which had once been part of human nature. Thus, the 'animality of madness' contributed to the notion of the 'immorality of the unreasonable' (Foucault, 1971). The horrific actions against this group were, therefore, regarded as acceptable. It was a period dominated by punishment rather than care, and as Foucault (1971) notes, the approach to the management of these groups was one that depicted them as being subject to unchained animality that could be mastered only by discipline and brutalizing. By the eighteenth century it was common to distinguish between the 'insane' and other 'problem populations', and by the mid-nineteenth century to incarcerate specific populations within the state-supported asylum system.

> The earliest of these were the small receptacle at Norwich, founded in 1713, and the ward for incurable lunatics established at Guy's Hospital in 1728. More important than these, inasmuch as it provided a model for other institutions established later in the century and also represented a major attempt to assert medical control over the problem of insanity, was the establishment of St Luke's Hospital in London in 1751. Subsequently, a second Luke's opened in 1764 at Newcastle upon Tyne, and in 1766 a 'lunatic hospital' with twenty-two cells opened in Manchester, attached to the existing Infirmary.

These were followed by similar institutions at York, Liverpool, Leicester, and Exeter. By the standards of the nineteenth century, none of these was a very large institution, and they never contained more than a minor portion of the insane population. (Scull, 1982: 25)

Madness was accepted to be a medical problem and the 'insane' were managed by the new population of 'mad-doctors' (Scull, 1982). The 'insane' were governed by the developing bureaucracies, and isolated physically and socially.

The medicalization of deviance and the 'insane' had parallels with the demands for the social control of an increasingly complex society. Scull (1982) has identified three main processes which secured the medical profession's claim to special expertise vis-à-vis the 'insane'. During the mid-nineteenth century there was increasing state involvement through rationalized administrations which formed part of the social control apparatus. The treatment of deviance was largely carried out within institutions, therefore, the segregation of 'deviants' from the community was able to be achieved. Lastly, there was a growing diversity of social action defined as deviant and administered by 'experts'. Insanity was one form of deviance, therefore, asylums and psychiatrists seemed essential and necessary. In his recent work, Scull (1993) traces the definition of madness during the eighteenth century providing evidence about the difference in this definition from the nineteenth century. This work reinforces the understanding of the increasing organization of the asylum system in England as one depicted by massive growth between 1847 and 1914, whereby the number of asylums increased from 21 to 97, with the number of 'lunatics' housed within these asylums increasing from approximately 500 to 108,000 over the same period (Scull, 1993). It was to this emerging secular religion of medicine that those individuals who starved themselves were increasingly confined.

The emergence of the clinic and its influence on modern procedures of hospitalization

The structural conditions of medicine and professional discourses about treatment construct a certain kind of treatment arena for anorexia nervosa. The historical emergence of the clinic is a key explanation of how the hospital became a 'taken-for-granted' system for the administration of health care. During the eighteenth century the emergence of the clinic related to changing social and political conditions, and its functions were separate from those of both the hospital and training medical personnel (Foucault, 1973). Most noteworthy was the change in the structure of 'medical perception' (Foucault, 1973). Although Foucault's analysis of the clinic is located within French history the changes in medical perception became common throughout Europe and the kind of clinic that Foucault describes was established in Britain during the 1770s (Cousins and Hussain, 1984). In the *Birth of the Clinic* (1973) Foucault describes two themes of medical thought, *medicine of species*, which was concerned with the classification of diseases, nosology and the treatment of individual patients, and *medicine of social spaces*, whereby the health of total populations became a concern at a national level. A major reason for this focus was the need for social organization to control and prevent infectious disease epidemics. This preventive focus later became instrumental in structuring a national health care system in England.

By the mid-eighteenth century onwards the medicine of social spaces became significant to the reorganization of medical experts and hospitals. Cousins and Hussain argue that for the individual this meant 'creating a model individual, conducting his [sic] life according to the precepts of health, and creating a medicalized society in order to bring the conditions of life and conduct in line with the requirements of health' (1984: 151). From this perspective it was necessary to define not only specific diseases that were potentially dangerous to populations but also behaviours that threatened social order. Individuals and groups who posed such a threat were segregated and removed from the general population and incarcerated within the clinic, asylum or prison. The clinic and asylum were sites of institutional confinement and contributed to the surveillance of populations. Prior to the French Revolution treatment within hospitals had been only one of its functions, it had also provided food and clothing for its 'pauper patients' (Foucault, 1973). Foucault argues that hospitals also had to undergo medicalization before they became the teaching and treating arenas with which we are now familiar. During the late eighteenth century French medical reforms involved the appointment of a commission in 1777 that together with the *Academie des Sciences* designed projects for hospital reform (Cousins and Hussain, 1984) and contributed to the process of what is now considered universally accepted medical training in hospitals.

The transformation in medical perception developed a shift away from the localization of diseases to the medical 'gaze' onto the body of the patient. Cousins and Hussain state that Foucault demonstrated how 'The emergence of anatomo-clinical medicine and what he calls "sciences of man" were more or less contemporaneous for in both of them Man [sic] is the subject and the object of knowledge' (1984: 167). Clearly, Foucault's (1973) analysis of the emergence of modern medicine, anatomo-clinical medicine, provides a socio-historical explanation of present day clinical practices. The hospital is not an institution that simply houses these practices, but is a form of institutional authority over its subjects; health care practitioners and patients, the site of teaching and patient management constructed through medical discourse.

From the late nineteenth century women have been subjects of experimental medical procedures involving immersion in cold baths, the administration of pills and tonics, and other solutions from apothecaries. Women who refused food were also segregated from public space during the nineteenth century. The middle class status of women documented in early diagnostic descriptions facilitated the practice of segregation because they afforded medical treatment and attendants within their own homes. Home confinement also transformed a woman's identity within the household from that of wife, or daughter, to a patient. Treatment within a residence converted the domestic sphere into an extension of space for medical practice that readily employed family members in the day-to-day surveillance of the woman's confinement. Since its initial discovery in 1874 the conceptualization of anorexia nervosa as a disease entity transformed the explanation of women who refused food through their position as subjects of clinical processes and objects of the medical gaze. Moreover, in the absence of an organic causation, physicians drew on the evolving field of psychiatry to define the cause of anorexia nervosa as a nervous disease. This definition secured the continued management of individuals within the medical arena, and the hospital facilitated the development and reproduction of clinical practices that are observable in modern eating disorder treatment units.

The transition from religious to medical authority

The social control and segregation of particular groups, such as women, is a long-standing practice related to the government and administration of populations. The religious establishment from the Middle Ages through to the eighteenth and nineteenth centuries increasingly constructed femininity as being essentially deviant and in opposition to the norms defined by the exclusively male elite group of clerics. This ideology, together with the increasing development of explanations of hysteria, became influential in later religious and medical thought and was significant in the conceptualization of madness. The negative view of women is supported by the overrepresentation of women in mental institutions dating back to the seventeenth century (cf. Showalter, 1987).

The previous sections describe how different interpretations of women and self-starvation existed during different historical periods and demonstrate the relationship of these interpretations to broader social and political ideas. The shift in ideas between the early religious interpretations of the twelfth and thirteenth centuries and the seventeenth and eighteenth centuries suggests that the later interpretations were linked with key ideas emerging through medicine and the transition from religious to medical scientific authority.

Self-starvation from the 1600s onwards

Later religious interpretations of self-starvation largely drew on the dichotomy that women were good or evil, as well as being interwoven with emerging medical interpretations and practices. Reports of women who were starving themselves during the seventeenth century and until the early nineteenth century continued a significant religious theme. For example, Jane Balan (1613) and Ann Moore (who claimed to have existed without nourishment between 1807 and 1813), were exposed as symbols of cunning and deceit (Brumberg, 1988). In a paper by Morgan (1977) he describes four examples of starving women including Jane Balan and Ann Moore. In 1613 Pedro Mexio described the case of Jane Balan who was known as the 'French Fasting Girl of Confolens', and who had lived during the late sixteenth century. Jane Balan was reported to have lived without any nourishment for three years. Her condition was attributed, in part, to the 'wicked power' which was contained in an apple given to her by a woman. Martha Taylor was reported in 1669 to have survived, again without food and drink, for thirteen months. Later accounts included those of Ann Moore, who was purported to have existed for six years without nourishment, and Sarah Jacob, who lived for two years, and who were regarded by clerics as evidence of women's existence through immortal intervention.

The earlier descriptions of self-starvation were attributed to a different religious interpretation than were later accounts. The later accounts have direct relevance to the view of women as being possessed by the devil. This could take the form of the woman who gave Jane Balan the apple which contained 'wicked power'. Starvation was fundamentally related to the negative spiritual state in women. Women's bodies were treated as especially threatening to the moral and social stability of society (Suleiman, 1986). According to traditional Christian religion the female body was thought to be 'A mysterious, unpredictable and even evil thing unless it was kept in its proper place and confined to its proper roles: chastity or incessant child bearing within marriage' (Szasz, 1971: 197).

The transition from religious to medical authority was a complex and vital process whereby the interests of particular dominant groups and the systems within which they lived were maintained. The definition and restraint of 'deviant' groups reinforced the need for social regulation. Szasz (1972) describes the development from religious to medical conceptions of madness in terms of 'rule-following behaviour'. The religious rules of life had disastrous effects for women in the form of witch-hunts, the identification of women as possessing evil spirits, and the notion that femininity was inherently wicked.

> We now deny moral, personal, political and social controversies by pretending that they are psychiatric problems; in short by playing the medical game. During the witch-hunts men denied these controversies by pretending that they were theological problems; in short by playing the religious game. (Szasz, 1972: 189)

Evidence of the transition from religious to medical authority over women is found in the later descriptions of starvation including the introduction of an increasingly scientific management of women. Reports state that Ann Moore and Sarah Jacob were continually observed by male physicians in an attempt to test the hypothesis that the women could continue a miraculous existence without nourishment. It was during these periods of surveillance that both women dramatically deteriorated and eventually died. These examples of women who are documented as starving themselves existed in a rich history prior to Gull's observations of women and the definition of self-starvation as anorexia nervosa. Some of the early medical definitions that also preceded Gull (1874) are found in the seventeenth and eighteenth centuries when physicians called self-starvation both 'inedia prodigiosa', a great starvation, and 'anorexia mirabilis', miraculously inspired loss of appetite (Brumberg, 1988). Morton (1694), also a physician, had attributed self-starvation to 'nervous atrophy'; a form of consumption which originated in the woman's 'ill and morbid state of the spirits'.

The common term to describe women like Ann Moore, was 'fasting girls', as Brumberg writes:

> the term 'fasting girl' was used by Victorians on both sides of the Atlantic to describe cases of prolonged abstinence where there was uncertainty about the etiology of the fast and ambiguity about the intention of the faster. (1988: 61)

Brumberg (1988) argues that the term 'fasting girls' mocked the tradition of asceticism and 'anorexia mirabilis'. She goes on to state that 'fasting girls' was the common term in public discussion even though 'anorexia mirabilis' appeared in medical dictionaries prior to the term anorexia nervosa. The work of Brumberg (1988) provides evidence of the colloquial use of physicians' language, which contributes to the interpretation of the emergence and uses of the language to describe particularly young women and self-starvation.

The latter reports of self-starvation and young women represent a change that marks the point of departure from a strictly religious to an increasing medical influence on ideas and the explanation of women. There was no clear conceptual separation between morality, religion and medicine, which formed a uniform system of social regulation (Turner, 1987). Religious and medical discourses, as well as their formulations of morality, did not displace each other within a specific period of time, but continued to exist as interrelational systems of knowledge.

The religious interpretation of women and self-starvation is significant to our contemporary understanding of anorexia nervosa because it demonstrates how self-starvation was explained differently over the course of several centuries prior to William Gull's definition in 1874. There is no single religious definition of women and self-starvation because women were interpreted differently during particular historical periods. The interpretations of self-starvation and women were made in relation to the changing nature of knowledge, such as the emerging concept of madness and the transition from religious to medical authority. Religious interpretation during the twelfth and thirteenth centuries is distinguished from later interpretations during the seventeenth century onwards by an interpretation of women's fasting as an ascetic pursuit. None of the religious eras can be seen as a true reflection of a religious interpretation, rather, each one represents the coalescence of several discourses that existed during particular historical periods. Part of later religious interpretation of women was based on the notion that women were possessed by the devil and the cause of many societal ills. This ideology, together with the increasing development of theories of hysteria, became influential in later medical thought and in the construction of women and madness.

An early and common medical explanation of the reported greater incidence of madness in women rather than men was attributed to the inheritance of insanity. This was a major argument of Darwinian psychiatrists. For example, Clouston (1911) argued that mothers had a greater tendency to transmit insanity to their female children. The association between female behaviours and madness became reproduced through dominant forms of knowledge that related specific feminine traits to the onset of psychopathology. During the late nineteenth century and the turn of the twentieth century the emergence of madness developed through the changing explanations of social groups, and particularly the professional interpretations of the nature of women. These interpretations heavily relied on notions of insanity and were constructed through discourses, or regular ways of organizing arguments and systems of thinking. In the following chapters some of these key discourses are discussed, and most importantly, the ways in which self-starvation became organized into a system of psychiatric thought and practice. Women, being the main group associated with self-starvation, became subjects of the emerging discourses of psychiatry, anorexia nervosa and the profound effects of these discourses, involving experimentation, social isolation, confinement and the continuing anomaly of psychological medicine.

2
The Late Nineteenth Century Medical Discovery of Anorexia Nervosa

Miss A., aet. 17, under the care of Mr. Kelson Wright, of the Clapham Road, was brought to me on Jan. 17, 1866. Her emaciation was very great. It was stated that she had lost 33 lbs. in weight. She was then 5st. 12 lbs. Height, 5 ft. 5 in. Amenorrhoea for nearly a year. No cough. Respirations throughout chest everywhere normal. Heart-sounds normal. Resp. 12; pulse, 56. No vomiting nor diarrhoea. Slight constipation. Complete anorexia for animal food, and almost complete anorexia for everything else. Abdomen shrunk and flat, collapsed. No abnormal pulsations of aorta. Tongue clean. Urine normal. Slight deposit of phosphates on boiling. The condition was one of simple starvation.

William W. Gull, 'Anorexia Nervosa (Apepsia Hysterica, Anorexia Hysterica)', *Transactions of the Clinical Society* (1874)

We know the images. They are familiar in all histories of psychiatry, where their function is to illustrate that happy age when madness was finally recognised and treated according to a truth to which we had too long remained blind.

Foucault, *Madness and Civilisation* (1971: 241)

Well over one hundred years have passed since the term 'anorexia nervosa' was first used to describe what was previously known as self-starvation. In 1874 Sir William Withey Gull defined his observations of the self-starvation of young women as anorexia nervosa. Meanwhile, his French contemporary, Dr E.C. Laseque, had referred to self-starvation as 'anorexie hysterique' in 1873, which became clinical usage in France and Italy. In this chapter I examine the medical discovery of anorexia nervosa by analysing the discourses that made such a discovery possible. My analysis is informed by Foucault's writings which I discussed in the introduction to the book, therefore, I was particularly concerned with the historical, social, and institutional conditions that made certain discourses possible and the subject positions made available to women. A discourse analysis of the historical construction of anorexia nervosa was first identified as being significant to contemporary understanding of the condition in a publication by Hepworth and Griffin (1990) and work by Hepworth (1991). This chapter is a slightly modified version of this earlier work and continues to be important because of the long-standing influence that Gull's writings have had on the developing explanations of anorexia nervosa. Following the analysis of historical discourse I discuss examples of medical writings on anorexia nervosa that appeared during the 1880s, subsequent to Gull's publications, in order to illustrate his influence in determining the naming and medical management of the condition.

The discourse of femininity

Anorexia nervosa was introduced into nineteenth century medical literature as an overwhelmingly female condition. As such, a critical analysis of
nineteenth century medical literature involves examining the social position
of women, and specifically middle class women, who became the most
common social group to be diagnosed with anorexia nervosa during this
period.

> The affluent woman of the late nineteenth century normally spent a hushed
> and peaceful life indoors, sewing, sketching, reading romances, planning
> menus, and supervising servants and children. Her clothes, a sort of portable
> prison of tight corsets and long skirts, prevented activity any more vigorous
> than a Sunday stroll. Society agreed that she was frail and sickly. Her delicate
> nervous system had to be shielded as carefully as her body, for the slightest
> shock could send her reeling off to bed. (Ehrenreich and English, 1978: 123)

During the latter half of the nineteenth century women's lives were
largely determined by societal expectations that they would take up their
'natural' domestic roles as wives and mothers. Women, as repositories of
the feminine, were not assumed to possess 'rational' knowledge, and were
thereby constructed through concepts that related to the explanation of
'irrationality'. Women's behaviours were often interpreted by physicians
and constructed in medical literature as 'deviant' (Ehrenreich and English,
1979). Anorexia nervosa provides one example of such an interpretation.
The construction of anorexia nervosa and diagnostic practices are also an
example of social processes that had serious implications for limiting the
representation of women and became functional in maintaining women's
subordination.

Drs W.W. Gull and E.C. Laseque have been credited, and have credited
themselves, with the 'discovery' of anorexia nervosa. Gull and Laseque
were physicians working in England and France respectively during the
latter half of the nineteenth century. Both men became known as authorities on the condition of anorexia nervosa as a result of their writings on a
small number of women who had been consulted by them or had been
brought to their attention by other physicians. Their writings about this
concept (anorexia nervosa) as a medical and moral condition associated
with women and the feminine tells us a great deal about nineteenth century
ideologies of femininity, disease and morality. First, however, it is necessary
to set the medical discourses of Gull and Laseque in context, and describe
the extent to which women were denied a social voice during the latter half
of the nineteenth century which made it possible to construct this discourse
of femininity. Within the dominant philosophical ideology of the time,
women in Western Europe were constructed as 'passive citizens' (Kennedy
and Mendus, 1989). 'Man' was synonymous with reason and logic: the norm
to which women could only aspire, whereas 'woman' was defined as the
'Other' and was seen to possess quite different qualities. The focus was also
on the elite class of women: this idealized form of femininity emphasized

fragility, passivity and irrationality as the 'natural' characteristics of white, upper and middle class women (Sayers, 1982).

There are two possible ways in which this articulation of women and the feminine came about. First, 'rationality' had become a highly valued attribute in Western societies through the emerging practice of science which aimed to uncover discoverable 'truths' about the world. Rationality was constructed as a specifically masculine intellectual quality, not least because the populations of scientists and theoreticians were almost exclusively male (Fee, 1981). Women were assumed to lack intellectual capability and were solely defined in terms of their domestic lives. Secondly, women were understood in terms of a specific epistemology which dominated Western thought. Nineteenth century empiricism and Cartesian dualism were central tenets of this 'rational method'. Dualism, usually associated with the separation of mind and body, structured theories and debates into separate and opposing constituent elements of dichotomies. The opposite of reason, logic and mindfulness was completely bestowed on women in their assumed possession of irrationality, and women's powerlessness as a social group enforced their practical and domestic existence.

The discourse of femininity associated specific qualities with the feminine, in direct opposition to those qualities and characteristics which were held to be synonymous with masculinity. The ideological representation of femininity constructed women as, 'emotional', 'creative', 'deviant' and 'mad', particularly when women's behaviour was construed as manifestations of hysteria, and compared with the 'rational', 'scientific' and 'logical' qualities of masculinity. William Gull expanded his interpretation of 'anorexia nervosa' as a specifically (or at least predominantly) female condition by arguing that this condition could be understood with reference to the available body of 'knowledge' about femininity and women. This 'knowledge' was profoundly ideological, but for Gull it held vital information about women's supposedly inherent irrationality which could be used to help him explain and understand anorexia nervosa. Both Gull's and Laseque's writings provide clear examples of how the construction of a specific ideology of femininity shaped the early medical management of women and in turn contributed to the reproduction of the social conditions of women. Anorexia nervosa was stated to be a female condition and was continually referred to as such throughout Gull's writings:

> I referred to a peculiar form of disease occurring mostly in young women, and characterised by extreme emaciation.... The subjects of this affection are mostly of the female sex, and chiefly between the ages of 16 and 23. (1874: 22)

Although, Gull (1874: 22) did state, 'I have occasionally seen it [anorexia] in males at the same age', this was his only reference to the incidence of anorexia in males. When male anorexia nervosa was addressed, Gull treated his observations with marginal importance. This intimate relationship between anorexia nervosa and women was related to the apparent complexity of the medical diagnosis, itself a result of the supposedly 'natural' irrationality of women. Gull constructed women as having an irrational disposition which could develop all too readily into conditions such as anorexia nervosa. Gull's French contemporary, E.C. Laseque, also introduced his audience to anorexia nervosa by emphasizing the gender-specific nature of the condition:

> The cases which have served me as a basis for this memoir are eight in number, all women, the youngest being 18, and the eldest 32. (1873: 368)

The memoir to which Laseque was referring was based on the description of a 'typical' case study, and he made no reference to the incidence of anorexia in males.

Both Gull and Laseque attempted to explain their observations of individual women by using the discourse of femininity in their development of an aetiology of anorexia nervosa. First, Gull and Laseque attempted to isolate a specific cause for this 'unusual' behaviour and this discourse was employed in connection with their observations of women's behaviour, as in the following:

> The patient complained of no pain, but was restless and active. This was in fact a striking expression of the nervous state, for it seemed hardly possible that a body so wasted could undergo the exercise which seemed agreeable. It is sometimes shocking to see the extreme exhaustion and emaciation of these patients brought for advice. (Gull, 1874: 23)

Gull's (1874) description of his observations of young women attached a sense of mystery to 'anorexic behaviour' by using terms such as 'hardly possible' and 'shocking'. The use of these descriptions made such behaviour seem unusual, and this served two possible functions. Anorexia nervosa was understood in medical literature in the context of the ideology of femininity and was seen as an extension of female irrationality. This context both obscured the scientific interpretation of anorexia nervosa and simultaneously limited other possible interpretations by marginalizing alternative arguments rehearsed over a century later by women who argue that anorexia nervosa is, for example, an aesthetic protest or act of resistance to dominant ideals.

In their search for an acceptable cause for anorexia nervosa, both Gull and Laseque heavily relied on the assumed 'irrational' nature of women, and especially young women, as a means of holding together their arguments. This was achieved through the association of the 'unusual' and 'irrational' in relation to women and anorexia nervosa, expressed in terms of 'mental perversion'. According to Gull:

> it will be admitted that young women at the ages named are specially obnoxious to mental perversity. (1874: 25)

and Laseque:

> it is now that is developed that perversion, which by itself is almost characteristic. (1873: 266)

> In comparing this satisfied assurance to the obstinacy of the insane, I do not think I am going too far. (1873: 367)

in fact, the whole disease is summed up in this intellectual perversion.
(1873: 368)

Gull (1874) addressed the mental state that could give rise to anorexia as
'mental perversion', and Laseque (1873) reinforced this notion by comparing anorexics to 'the insane'. However, the nineteenth century use of 'perversion' was related to obstinacy and stubbornness unlike twentieth century
usage in relation to, for example, 'sexual perversion' and deviance. This
obstinacy was seen as being characteristic of the irrationality of insanity and
women during the late nineteenth century. Thus, the articulation of anorexia
nervosa and women also drew on the emerging notion of an inherently
female madness, and that together, they were functional in developing the
idea that female madness could develop into specific nervous diseases. This
argument had been similarly used in the explanation of 'hysteria' and
'neurasthenia' (cf. Showalter, 1987). By grounding anorexia nervosa in the
discourse of femininity, Gull and Laseque were able to present such 'mental
perversion' as a state which was only to be expected of young women, who
were, after all, inherently irrational and emotionally unstable. This explanation formed the basis of a developing aetiology of anorexia nervosa which
was influential due to the scientific and medical context within which it was
discussed, and to the status of the observers as respected physicians.

The discourse of discovery

Descriptions of food refusal that resemble anorexia nervosa have been
recorded from as early as the twelfth and thirteenth centuries, and were
understood primarily within the religious sphere. Historical assumptions
about the existence of an essential female nature were integral to the new
explanation of the act of food refusal by women defined through medical
interpretation as anorexia nervosa. While the medical discovery of anorexia
nervosa was overwhelmingly documented as being based on scientific
knowledge, morality was central to this construction, and is discussed later.
Gull's repeated references to the point at which the discovery of anorexia
nervosa emerged had two main consequences. First, the independence of
his work was emphasized, since this marked anorexia nervosa out as a condition which had been discovered and was exclusive to Gull. Second, a
strong link with medical science was established because Gull was writing
as a physician, despite the fact that the contribution of medical science to
the explanation of anorexia nervosa was minimal, it marked an official shift
away from the religious discourse. Gull insisted that his discovery was made
independently:

> After these remarks were penned, Dr. Francis Webb directed my attention to
> the paper of Dr. Laseque ... Dr. Laseque does not refer to my address at
> Oxford, and it is most likely he knew nothing of it. There is, therefore, the more
> value in this Paper, as our observations have been made independently.
> (1874: 25)

Gull repeatedly drew attention to the way in which his work had developed in comparison to Laseque's, but emphasized that the research writings were in no way connected. Gull aimed to reinforce his status as the discoverer of anorexia nervosa in Britain:

> It is plain that Dr. Laseque and I have the same malady in mind, though the forms of our illustrations are different. . . . We have both selected the same expression to characterise the malady. (1874: 25)

Gull did acknowledge that his French contemporary was working on 'the same malady', which in a sense, deflected some of the kudos for the discovery of anorexia nervosa away from Gull. Because of Laseque's work, Gull lost all sight of making anorexia nervosa exclusively a British medical discovery, and of making himself the person responsible for its formal documentation. This is a familiar part of the pressure to gain individual recognition for scientific attainment that continues in the late twentieth century. The discourse of discovery is still very pervasive and many similar examples can be found in contemporary scientific practice (Mulkay et al., 1982).

However, following this recognition of Laseque's work, Gull introduced an interesting change to the terminology of anorexia nervosa. While he used the term 'apepsia hysterica' in his initial discussion of anorexia in 1868, Gull had changed this to 'anorexia nervosa' by 1874:

> In the address at Oxford, I used the term "Apepsia Hysterica", but before seeing Dr. Laseque's paper it had equally occurred to me that "Anorexia" would be more correct. (1874: 25)

Gull chose anorexia nervosa as a 'more correct' term and, again, assured his audience of the independence of his conclusion from Laseque's work. At this point Gull established the term anorexia nervosa, which has continued to date as the diagnostic term, and Gull is now credited as the person who 'coined the term' (Palmer, 1980). Gull emphatically stated that this change occurred prior to reading Laseque's (1873) work where Laseque had used the term 'hysterical anorexia'. Gull's initiative in renaming the condition anorexia nervosa emphasized his role in the discovery of the apparently new medical condition. The discovery of anorexia nervosa can be explained in a less glamorous way as part of a competition between Gull and Laseque for a secure position as one of the nineteenth century's Great Men of Science. The justifications for each of the three terms were not discussed at any length, being largely based on descriptive case study material, and the failure of successive medical hypotheses.

Anorexia, in a literal sense, means 'loss of appetite', which was not always contingent upon documenting the presentation and diagnosing the condition anorexia nervosa identified by Gull and Laseque. Nervosa is a broad term used extensively in the nineteenth century as the complexity of anatomical functioning became more apparent, and the relationship between mind and body was beginning to be articulated within the emerging science of psychopathology. However, the dominant interpretations of the term nervosa are medical, and when attributed to anorexia had the effect of classifying the condition as a 'nervous disease'. This served to pathologize the condition, and reinforce the use of medical scientific and clinical discourses in its documentation and management.

The medical scientific discourse

Gull's (1874) paper on anorexia nervosa represented his attempts to explain a condition through its categorization and integration into a medical paradigm. As medical 'experts', male physicians contrasted their own supposedly rational attempts to explain the condition with the irrational nature of female anorexic symptomatology. Moreover, the medical paradigm rested on a discourse of scientific discovery which searched for the organic causes of specific medical conditions in order to arrive at a diagnosis (Gilbert and Mulkay, 1984). Gull attempted to find a specific cause for the condition he called anorexia nervosa using the traditional medical model:

> I remarked that at present our diagnosis of this affection is negative so far as determining any positive cause from which it springs. (1874: 22)

> There was some peevishness of temper and feeling of jealousy. No account could be given of the exciting cause. (1874: 23)

> The patient, who was a plump, healthy girl until the beginning of last year (1887), began early in February, without apparent cause, to evince a repugnance to food. (1888: 516)

When the search became unsuccessful, Gull argued that anorexia nervosa resisted further definition. At this point Gull started to move away from his search for an organic aetiology and began to look towards the psyche. Rather than admitting that the formalization of anorexia nervosa within the medical scientific paradigm was under question, Gull used the lack of causation to further justify an appeal to the 'peculiar' nature of female anorexia nervosa. It should not be assumed that Gull and Laseque's arguments followed a linear path, nor that each discourse was presented in sequential fashion within their texts. Their failure to identify an organic cause of anorexia nervosa did produce a shift towards the psychological domain in search of an explanation, but these themes formed a cyclical rather than a linear pattern. Gull continued to search for organic causes, even though he was beginning to suggest that anorexia nervosa originated from 'mental perversion':

> In the stage of greatest emaciation one might have been pardoned for assuming that there was some organic lesion, but (from the point of view indicated) such an assumption would have been unnecessary. (1874: 23)

> Death apparently followed from starvation alone. (1874: 24)

> I have not observed in these cases any gastric disorder to which the want of appetite could be referred. I believe, therefore, that its origin is central and not peripheral. (1874: 25)

Gull (1874) eventually abandoned the possible organic (peripheral) causation and strongly attributed anorexia nervosa to the patient's mental state (central origin). His attempts to explain anorexia nervosa using the organic reading of the medical scientific discourse had seemingly failed. Throughout Gull's (1874) paper these attempts became increasingly futile as he reported the rejection of several medical hypotheses. Although his explanation for anorexia nervosa shifted from the organic and physiological to the psychological, it remained firmly within the medical scientific discourse.

> The want of appetite is, I believe, due to a morbid mental state. (Gull, 1874: 25)

> This story, in fine, is an illustration of most of these cases, perversions of the 'ego' being the cause and determining the course of the malady. (Gull, 1874: 25)

The ideas and concepts of nineteenth century psychological speculation were reflected in the use of terms such as morbid mental state. Gull frequently employed the term 'perversion' within a psychological framework, but in the context of a search for the cause of anorexia nervosa and his attempts to develop diagnostic criteria along medical lines. These writings are an example of the medicalization of the psychological domain. This process was achieved by interpreting psychological phenomena within similar medical frameworks used to interpret organic phenomena. The process of medicalization was not confined to anorexia nervosa since it has permeated ideologies of mental health and shaped the health care institutions of the twentieth century (cf. Foucault, 1971). Gull eventually concluded that anorexia nervosa was caused by 'perversions of the ego'. This was Gull's final conclusion which became frequently quoted by his colleagues, and was a conclusion that was largely derived from the continued notion of the inherently irrational nature of women.

Laseque also made this move into the psychological realm. He wrote about anorexia nervosa as an exclusively female condition, arguing that the cause lay in women's emotional and unstable nature. Laseque rested his explanation of anorexia nervosa on supposed disturbances in women's marital, sexual and emotional lives. In this context, anorexia nervosa could not be presented as a reflection of the nature of women's social position, but rather a result of the failure of individual young middle class women to move without fuss into their pre-ordained marital and domestic roles. According to Laseque:

> Generally it relates to some real or imaginary marriage project, to a violence done to some sympathy, or to some more or less conscient desire. (1873: 265)

Women were discouraged from intellectual stimulation, and were commonly 'prescribed' enforced passivity, limited reading and advised to lead a quiet, domestic life, after being diagnosed as anorexic or 'hysterical' (cf. Showalter, 1987). Laseque wrote that:

> what dominates in the mental condition of the hysterical patient is, above all the state of quietude – I might also say a condition of contentment truly pathological. (1873: 367)

Hysteria, anorexia nervosa and other terms were often used inter-changeably as seen in this text. Laseque also emphasizes the quietude/con-tentment of his patient that he goes on to attribute to a pathological cause. In contrast to this Gull (1874: 23) described his patients' agitation which is consistent with the dominant representations of hysterical women during the nineteenth century portrayed as being uncontrollable. Women were also prescribed passivity in the form of, for example, the rest cure, which seems incongruous with their perceived state of pathological con-tentment by Laseque. In developing the aetiology of anorexia nervosa, these writings further served to reinforce the association between women, femininity, irrationality and madness. Whilst the diagnosis of anorexia nervosa was most often discussed through the medical scientific discourse, the various treatments for this 'new condition' were to be found within the clinical discourse.

The clinical discourse

The use of medical knowledge to explain the aetiology of anorexia nervosa increasingly suggested that there was no organic causation and the docu-mentation of anorexia nervosa as a medical condition seemed inappropri-ate. However, the realization of the limitations of the medical scientific paradigm were articulated in a particular way that permitted the 'anorexic condition' to maintain a continuous medical connection being successfully established through the clinical discourse. This connection was developed through decisions that were made in relation to what prescriptive treat-ments were suitable for anorexia nervosa, even though such medical treat-ments lacked any definite curative properties. Gull admitted there was a marked absence of any relationship between the medical preparations pre-scribed and the patient's recovery from anorexia nervosa:

> Various remedies were prescribed – the preparation of cinchona, the bichlo-ride of mercury, syrup of the phosphate of iron, citrate of quinine and iron – but no perceptible effect followed their administration. (1874: 23)

> The medical treatment probably need not be considered as contributing much to the recovery. (1874: 24)

> by warmth and steady supplies of food and stimulants, the strength may be gradually resuscitated, and recovery completed. (1874: 25)

The essential prescription for recovery was based solely on warmth, food and stimulants (tonics). The physician's objective was to establish normal body weight and metabolic rate, so that the body could function effectively. This medical treatment is more usually used as a response to malnutrition.

The historical inequities in power within the physician–patient relation-ship, where the physician occupies the autonomous position and the patient is positioned as the subject of medical processes, was a further process that facilitated the connection between anorexia nervosa and medicine. Despite the failure of the medical scientific paradigm to determine a causation for anorexia nervosa, women were managed within the spaces created by the emerging professionalization of medicine which structured arenas to manage illness and regulate abnormal behaviour. These arenas functioned through the clinical discourse in different ways. In relation to anorexia nervosa this usually meant that male physicians had complete control over female patients. This relationship formed an integral part of the medical process, involving diagnosis, intervention and treatment, all of which were subsumed under the notion that a cure for each medical condition was discoverable.

Davis (1988) writes that within such a relationship the need to control the patient is constantly present, for she has relinquished a degree of autonomy, and finds herself 'managed' within the medical domain. Control of the patient is an integral part of the doctor–patient relationship, because it allows the medical process to function with relative ease. Contemporary analyses of (male) doctor–patient (female) relationships indicate that such interactions frequently resemble a process of negotiation, but in which the doctor has greater institutional power (Fisher and Todd, 1983). The practice of negotiation between the doctor and patient, especially within psychiatry, is relatively recent and should not be assumed to be common to all institutions. In the historical writings of both Gull and Laseque, we can see that the notion of patient autonomy was significant in patient management and treatment concerns, when particularly Gull warned against allowing the patient any autonomy as this may compromise her recovery:

> Food should be administered at intervals varying inversely with the exhaustion and emaciation. The inclination of the patient must be in no way consulted. (1874: 24)

> The restless activity referred to is also to be controlled, but this is often difficult. (1874: 25)

While medical treatments were repeatedly tried with the presentation of anorexia nervosa as a means of alleviating the condition, it became increasingly apparent that medical treatment was being rendered ineffective. The patient was not consulted, neither was any effective communication established, nor even thought desirable. In Gull's move away from attempts to determine an organic cause for anorexia nervosa, and the redirection of his attention towards the psyche, treatment and control of this condition also changed. The form of knowledge had changed from medical science to the rapidly developing discipline of psychiatry: 'The treatment required is obviously that which is fitted for persons of unsound mind' (Gull, 1874: 25).

Gull concluded that the origin of anorexia nervosa was 'central and not peripheral' thus treatments for a condition that was regarded as a manifestation of psychopathology were swiftly employed. It is important to note that Gull's conclusion marked a crucial moment in recording anorexia nervosa in medical and psychiatric literature, and his 1874 paper has proven to be most influential in directing the course of enquiry and clinical management. The movement towards a psychiatric perspective included the assumption that in treating the 'central' origin of anorexia nervosa, a similar epistemology could be used to that which treated the body. In other words, the medical process of diagnosis, intervention and treatment was applied to the psyche with the overall aim of regulating and controlling the patient. The status of nineteenth century medical science was so great that the psychological domain was constructed as appropriate subject matter for medical procedures. Foucault argues that during the eighteenth century there was no differentiation between 'physical medicaments and moral treatments and it was not yet accepted as obvious by medical thought' (1973: 178). This differentiation was beginning to be made through the clinical discourse of the late nineteenth century. According to Gull:

> The patient should be fed at regular intervals, and surrounded by persons who would have moral control over them; relations and friends being generally the worst attendants. (1874: 26)

and Laseque:

> When, after several months, the family, the doctor, and the friend perceive the persistent inutility of all these attempts, anxiety and with it moral treatment commences. (1873: 266)

Gull and Laseque were referring here to early practices of psychiatric control over patients. The introduction of 'moral control' and 'moral treatment' received much attention from the medical profession as instruments which could be employed by physicians in the emerging arena of 'mental illness'.

The relationship between medicine and morality has a long history. The moral treatment of anorexia nervosa was chosen not least because of its religious connections. Also, medicine and religion enjoyed prestigious and complementary social positions. Moral treatment, an instrument that was presumed to offer a renewal of spirit to the inflicted, became the common method with which to rectify the anorexic's behaviour. Anorexia nervosa, in becoming regarded as another form of insanity, was anticipated to respond to treatment, and anorexics' 'irrational' behaviour would benefit from moral treatment. Moral treatment was based on a belief that the 'lunatic' would be transformed, or as Scull (1982) notes, it was employed to remodel the 'lunatic' into something approximating the bourgeois ideal of the rational mind. Isolation was seen as being a necessary part of moral treatment and argued to be beneficial to the patient, as reflected in both Gull's and Laseque's observations that the anorexic's interaction with family and friends was futile, if not intrusive and debilitating. Therefore, isolation from personal influences was prescribed together with specifically chosen 'moral attendants'. The objective was to assimilate madness in all its manifestations, such that 'anorexic behaviour' was to be treated by the removal of 'anorexic' women from the social world, and through their education in moral rectitude.

The discourse of hysteria

The medical scientific discourse was beginning to be used alongside another; the discourse of hysteria. Foucault (1971) in writing about hysteria distinguishes between three eras. Hysteria became mostly associated with nervous diseases and madness through the third era that was depicted by 'an ethic of nervous sensibility' (Foucault, 1971: 146). This era translated the association between hysteria and madness differently from the early period of eighteenth century classical madness and material causes. Hysteria, observed and recorded by physicians in the latter nineteenth century, was regarded as a psychological effect of moral fault. The interpretation of madness became focused on the unconscious and the scientifically unobservable, as Foucault (1971) writes, eventually collapsing and spreading over the surface of a domain:

> psychology and morality would soon occupy together and contest with each other. The 'scientific psychiatry' of the nineteenth century became possible. It was in these 'diseases of the nerves' and in these 'hysterias', which would soon provoke its irony, that this psychiatry took its origin. (Foucault, 1971: 158)

The significance of the reference to hysteria here is twofold in terms of the ways in which 'hysteria' and 'nervousness' were related, and how these ideas became a dominant explanation of female abnormal behaviour. First, the link between women and hysteria had an established history, and had been used throughout several centuries as a means of explaining women's behaviour by the religious establishment. The medical and psychiatric professions employed hysteria in explanatory frameworks. Since anorexia nervosa was predominantly found in women, the association with hysteria became an obvious explanatory tool for Gull and Laseque.

The late nineteenth century, specifically between 1870 and 1914, has been called 'the golden age of hysteria' (Showalter, 1987: 129). During this period, hysteria became more specific in its application to women, which coincided with the beginnings of the women's emancipation movement. Sayers (1982) has argued that women's demands for emancipation coincided with various attempts to discredit their demands from patriarchal institutions which employed academic and scientific terms in their arguments in an attempt to give them a patina of respectability. Middle class, white women were becoming increasingly organized in their struggle for education, and women's so-called 'nervous diseases' were also reported to be increasing. 'Hysteria', 'neurasthenia' and 'anorexia nervosa' all became commonly identified as specific to women and were fundamentally related to their natural, 'hysterical' disposition. The symptoms common to all three conditions included blushing, vertigo, headaches and refusing to eat (Showalter, 1987).

Second, the connection between hysteria and anorexia nervosa was functional in maintaining a psycho-medical framework. The shift from the organic to the psychological in the search for a cause of anorexia nervosa was partly managed through the discourse of hysteria. The construction of hysteria has played a central role in the pathologizing of womanhood and femininity from the mid-nineteenth century (Foucault, 1971). It is possible that anorexia nervosa was perceived as being based on psychopathology because it had been regarded along with hysteria. Hysteria had already been constructed as a way of explaining the mind and its relationship to psychosomatic illness. This enabled physicians to articulate the condition as having psychological (central) origin and as such they wrote about the effects of 'mental perversions'. The use of the discourse of hysteria to explain anorexia nervosa in women was based on several assumptions that male physicians made about the putative cause of many psychological and physical ailments in women, and were strongly reinforced and popularized by Freud.

The association between anorexia nervosa and hysteria developed as the dominant means of explaining food refusal in women. Gull's 1868 paper initially referred to the condition of 'hysteria apepsia', and his original hypothesis was that hysteria had caused a pepsin imbalance which led to anorexia. Gull never elaborated on this supposed relationship, although he did mention some reservations about the relevance of hysteria to anorexia, admitting that in many cases there was an absence of hysterical symptomatology.

Gull tried to avoid addressing this confusion by arguing that the actual use of the term 'hysteria' was not necessarily based on the observation of hysterical symptoms in his 'subjects': 'We might call the state hysterical without committing ourselves to the etymological value of the word, or maintaining that the subjects of it have the common symptoms of hysteria' (1874: 25). Although Gull frequently used medical terms such as 'mesenteric disease', hysteria was increasingly employed in its classical sense, whereby hysteria was thought to affect a part of the body and cause psychosomatic illness. In the quote below, Laseque states that anorexia was a result of a gastric disorder. Throughout, anorexia nervosa was seen as being an individualistic condition, either in terms of individual psychopathology, or as a hysterical reaction to some external and self-imposed preoccupation, such as Laseque's (1873: 265) 'real or imaginary marriage projects'. Laseque argued that there was a direct causal relationship between anorexia and hysteria, advocating the need to maintain a strong connection with the medical scientific discourse:

> The terms 'anorexia' might have been replaced by 'hysterical inanition', which would better represent the most characteristic of the incidents, but I have preferred the former term . . . because it refers to a phenomenology which is less superficial, more delicate, and also more medical. The object of this memoir is to make known one of the forms of hysteria of the gastric centre. (1873: 265)

Laseque was convinced, unlike Gull, that hysteria had a definite relationship with anorexia, and that a medical explanation could clarify that relationship. It is clear that Laseque's argument was similar to Gull's initial hypothesis, that anorexia was caused by a gastric disorder, yet he too moved swiftly into the psychological domain. The discourse of hysteria, like the medical scientific discourse, allowed Laseque and Gull to make this discursive shift. For Laseque: '[Mental] perversion justifies the name which I have proposed for want of a better – hysterical anorexia' (1873: 265). Laseque, in common with Gull, used 'mental perversion' frequently as an interchangeable term with which to discuss 'hysterical anorexia'. This established a relationship between 'mental illness', anorexia nervosa and hysteria, all of which were constructed as being common in women. In this case it was the discourse of femininity which bound these elements so closely together wherein the discourse of hysteria became functional in the interpretation and management of women and their social world.

The moment at which anorexia nervosa emerged was not an example of individual human action that revealed a hitherto unknown medical condition. Rather, it formed part of the process through which states of food refusal, previously understood and dealt with in the religious realm, came to be medicalized through the terminology and treatment of anorexia nervosa. The discovery of anorexia nervosa was crucial to the process of medicalization, and the somewhat lengthy confusion over the precise name and cause of this 'new' medical condition reflected the considerable difficulties faced by male physicians in constructing criteria for diagnosis and treatment. Physicians like Gull and Laseque complained that the peculiarly female and irrational nature of anorexia nervosa rendered it inexplicable to the male rational mind. It is ironic that they then managed to construct themselves as 'experts' on this 'new' condition. During this period it was unthinkable that these young female patients should or could be treated as reliable sources of information on their own experiences.

The discourse of femininity used by Gull and Laseque had obvious ideological resonances, but it also had implications for women on a material level. There is a major contradiction in the texts of Laseque and Gull. Young women were berated on the one hand for being too agitated and 'restless', and on the other for being too 'contented'. Once women were being observed within the medical domain, however, to a large degree all behaviours and actions could be defined as being symptomatic of anorexia nervosa through the medical scientific discourse. This has similarities with contemporary definitions of young women who are explained using ambiguous frameworks. For example, young women who are defined as 'at risk' within the social or youth work context, as either too heterosexual, or not heterosexual enough (Marchant and Smith, 1977; Griffin, 1982). Both sets of apparently contradictory 'symptoms' of anorexia nervosa were pathologized as being manifestations of hysteria. The ideology of femininity sets a series of traps from which there is no apparent escape; problems for which there are no acceptable solutions.

Further historical references to anorexia nervosa: the 1890s

There are numerous references to self-starvation that later became known as anorexia nervosa. Although one of the earliest reports of a condition resembling anorexia nervosa was written by Richard Morton in 1694, in *A Nervous Consumption*, it was William Gull's (1874) writings that became a catalyst for British physicians to begin to name their observations of self-starvation as anorexia nervosa. Interestingly, during the 1890s some of the observations of young girls and women began to be reported in medical literature as retrospective cases of anorexia nervosa. Dr W.J. Collins wrote in *The Lancet* on 27 January 1894, about a young girl of seven and a half years old who had refused food for ten weeks, comparing her with Gull's case descriptions of anorexia nervosa. Collins wrote of the young girl's recovery, which, like the majority of Gull's cases, had occurred over the course of weeks. The example below is of a description of a recovery following nine weeks of hospitalization:

> Massage with neat's-foot oil, a copious dietary, cod-liver oil, and some liquor pancreaticus constituted the physical treatment. Her condition immediately began to improve, and with increasing weight and the restored use of her limbs her mental and moral state completely changed. (Collins, 1894: 202)

Unlike Collins' comparison with Gull's reports, which had focused on recovery, Mr Lockhart Stephens, describes a fatality resulting from anorexia nervosa in *The Lancet* on 5 January 1895. Similarly, Lockhart Stephens refers to the cases 'under the care of the late Sir William Gull', and remarks that 'the disease does not often prove fatal' which, for Stephens, led him to regard his example of 'considerable importance'.

> A girl sixteen years of age was admitted to the Emsworth Cottage Hospital on March 10th, 1888, on account of extreme emaciation. . . . I advised her parents to allow her to come into the Cottage Hospital on the distinct understanding and promise that whatever treatment was thought necessary should be carried out. She was ordered to be kept in bed with her limbs and body bandaged in cotton wool, to be fed every four hours with peptonised food, and to do nothing in the way of exertion. (Stephens, 1895: 31)

On 3 April 1888 the young woman under the care of Stephens died. Lockhart Stephens makes no further deliberations about the psychology of the patient with the following third of his article reporting the anatomical findings from the autopsy.

On 10 May 1890, an eleven year old girl was admitted to the North Eastern Children's Hospital, England. During the preceding week the girl's history was reported as one week's loss of flesh, anorexia and vomiting. For four years the girl had had similar 'attacks', but these had been intermittent. Dr C.F. Marshall had been the physician under whose care she had been placed in 1890. In response to the article by Stephens in 1895 about a fatal case of anorexia nervosa, in an article published in the subsequent issue of *The Lancet* Marshall wrote about the girl's fatality:

> As she refused all food she was fed on enemata of peptonised milk, beef tea, and brandy. In two or three days peptonised milk and beef tea were taken by the mouth in small and frequent doses. In ten days she could take a moderate diet by the mouth, but suffered from diarrhoea. On the thirteenth day after admission she rapidly became worse, the temperature rose to 102°F., and on the fifteenth day she died. (1895: 149–50)

The majority of these reports are of very young girls aged from seven through to sixteen, which is different from the ages reported in late twentieth century literature as being from mid-teens through to early twenties. These medical reports and observations of self-starvation became commonly known as cases of anorexia nervosa and illustrate the increasingly common usage of the diagnosis in Britain during the 1890s.

Reference to anorexia nervosa did not appear in the United States until 1893 (Vandereycken and Lowenkopf, 1990), when an article was published in the *The American Journal of the Medical Sciences* by James Hendrie Lloyd, who described a case of 'Hysterical tremor and hysterical anorexia of a severe type'. The case description was of a twenty six year old woman from the countryside in Pennsylvania who became ill in 1890:

> Her appearance was sufficient proof that her stomach received and digested the smallest amount of food necessary for life. (Lloyd, 1893: 274; quoted in Vandereycken and Lowenkopf, 1990: 533)

James Hendrie Lloyd wrote of treating this case and her subsequent recovery from anorexia nervosa in the following passage:

> The secret of success in treating the case was in removing the patient from her home, putting her under a good nurse, and using tact, encouragement, food, and good *morale*, with very little medicine. (1893: 276; quoted in Vandereycken and Lowenkopf, 1990: 534)

The first Australian case description of anorexia nervosa was described by the physician H.E. Astles in 1882 (Vandereycken and Beumont, 1990). This case description was located in South Australia, and particularly mentions the locality of Port Elliot, a small coastal resort. Dr Astles wrote:

> I was called to see a young lady 22 years of age, who through extreme exhaustion had been unable for some days to leave her bed. I found the case to be one typical of starvation. Complained of no pain. Pulse, 56; temperature, nearly a degree below normal. Respiration slow, but nothing could be detected that pointed to visceral disease. The parents simply stated their inability to get their daughter to eat, and this state had existed for many months. There was a decided expression of hysteria, from which I found most members of the family suffered. I prescribed the brandy and egg mixture of the pharmacopoea to be taken as medicine, and, also, the use of nutrient enemata. (Astles, 1882: In Vandereycken and Beumont, 1990: 109)

Dr Astles continued:

> I watched this case for several weeks and feeling that drugs were of but little avail, and that her best chance of recovery rested on her removal from home sympathy and influences, I persuaded the parents to send her to Port Elliot, and there in the house of a stranger she rapidly recovered. (Astles 1882; quoted in Vandereycken and Beumont, 1990: 109)

These early medical responses to two cases of anorexia nervosa have similarities in both the nature of the treatment that was prescribed; removal of the women from their homes and their relocation, and the observation of recovery from anorexia nervosa subsequent to their relocation. A contemporary term for similar events has been called a 'parentectomy' (Vandereycken et al., 1989). In the report by Lockhart Stephens, it is interesting to note that he had concluded, prior to reading Gull's article on anorexia nervosa, that the young woman under his care was a case of 'voluntary starvation'. On reading Gull's articles, Stephens attributed the starvation to the condition known as anorexia nervosa. William Gull's discovery of anorexia nervosa greatly stimulated late nineteenth century medical writing about self-starvation. Physicians compared their observations of young women and self-starvation with Gull's writings to establish their diagnoses of this medical phenomenon.

The legacy of late nineteenth century psychiatry

During the late nineteenth century anorexia nervosa had become formalized as a psychiatric condition and for this reason numerous attempts were made to find a successful treatment. Because of the classification of anorexia nervosa as a mental disorder, patients became the recipients of various treatment methods that reflected the developing science of psychiatry. However, from the turn of the century until the 1930s there were few reports about anorexia nervosa, which, in part, is explained by the associations made with the description of 'Simmonds' disease'. This disease was first described by Simmonds in 1914, typified by pituitary cachexia, involved patients significantly abstaining from food, and may have represented a proportion of previously diagnosed cases of anorexia nervosa. Simmonds' disease was thought at this time to be the cause of anorexia nervosa. The emerging scientific basis of psychiatry had the effect of proposing various hypotheses about the origins and treatment of anorexia nervosa and patients diagnosed with this disease became subject to experimental ideas. In this section I summarize some of the treatment interventions used during the height of this period of experimentalism.

Reference to anorexia nervosa from the 1930s to the 1950s

Reports during the 1930s in Britain, such as the article by Dr J.A. Ryle in *The Lancet*, on 17 October 1936, continued the tradition of acknowledging Gull's original work as the basis for diagnosing and treating self-starvation as anorexia nervosa. Ryle's article illustrates the development of psychiatric medicine and the early differentiation of anorexia nervosa in relation to younger and older women, men, and the appearance of psychotic symptomatology, which would render it a psychoneurosis. This is one of the first examples of how anorexia nervosa became an object of further investigation in terms of its classification within the continuing framework of nosology in medical science. During the first half of the twentieth century many of the psychiatric treatments reflected the increasing employment of scientific practices in managing mental illness. The introduction of medical technologies dominated psychiatric treatments and a number of non-reversible interventions were trialed with anorexic patients. These interventions included prefrontal lobotomy and leucotomy (Nemiah, 1958), and later interventions included insulin therapy and electroconvulsive therapy. The 1930s and 1940s abound with references to women diagnosed with psychiatric illnesses such as schizophrenia and chronic depression. The resurgence of interest in 'nervous diseases' is attributable in part to these new technologies of psychiatry. Also, the concept of insanity was undergoing a change during this time: while retaining the central notion of pathology, researchers searched for scientific evidence of a biological foundation to psychological dysfunction and this often meant attempting to measure the effects of psychiatric interventions. In England the three most common treatments for psychiatric conditions considered to be intractable were insulin shock therapy, electroconvulsive therapy and lobotomy.

While the early part of the twentieth century is certainly a period in which abhorrent treatment practices were used with individuals diagnosed with anorexia nervosa, there were some exceptions to this movement. American physician, John C. Nemiah, provides an excellent overview of early twentieth century American psychiatry and anorexia nervosa in his 1958 paper. There are two particularly interesting points in this work. First, Nemiah refers to Gull's nineteenth century treatment plan; a plan that is characterized by the simple provision of nourishing stimulants and observation, that Nemiah states has been little improved on since. Second, Nemiah was clearly emphasizing the conservative use of invasive treatment procedures, namely psychosurgery, force feeding and physical restraints that kept the patient in bed to maximize weight gain. Given the rise in scientific rationalism that depicted the approach to mental illness during the 1930s and 1950s, it is surprising to note such a response, and that Nemiah did not consider Gull's early therapies naïve.

A different view of anorexia nervosa is found in an article published in the *British Medical Journal* (1956). Hawkings et al. (1956) defined individuals who refused food within a category of 'deliberate disability'. The authors describe their interpretations in the following passage:

> We have become interested in a group of patients whose deceits in the medical sphere contrast with their conscientious attitude in other respects and whose disability, unlike that of most malingerers and many hysterics, is not directed to immediate gain or advantage. We were also struck by their close resemblance to patients suffering from anorexia nervosa, and felt that further study might cast indirect light upon the difficult problem of the wilful rejection of food. (Hawkings et al., 1956: 361)

A group of individuals, nineteen in total, had presented at various Departments of the United Birmingham Hospitals, England, UK, due to deliberate injury or illness. Two of the nineteen were recorded as suffering from anorexia nervosa, while the others were described as presenting with 'the difficult problem of the wilful rejection of food', which the authors aimed to investigate. Of particular interest is the way in which the researchers wrote about the notion of self-infliction by drawing on the social and cultural conditions of the period in which the article was written. During the 1950s self-inflicted injuries were regarded as manifestations of psychopathology, yet the researchers acknowledge specific social conditions that led to self-inflicted injuries. Writing during the period of post-war Britain, the researchers compared the group of nineteen patients, of whom none had apparent gain from their disability, with the occurrence of self-inflicted injuries by soldiers who had inflicted their injuries in order to be released from military service. In making this comparison the researchers separated civilian from military patients due to the different interpretations of the deliberate nature of the injuries. This separation reinforced the notion that self-inflicted disability resulted from psychopathology because the researchers could not perceive any reason for the behaviour outside of the military context. The article concludes by stating that the majority of the patients go on to do well and become 'useful and effective rather than neurotic and dependent members of society', and in the process they justify their administration of treatments, 'despite the deliberately produced nature of their lesions'.

This article reveals a moralistic aspect to the definition of different illnesses and different patient populations. To some extent this morality continues in attitudes towards women who refuse food through disparaging approaches to individuals who are defined as suffering 'self-inflicted' conditions. Illness that is considered in this way has serious implications for individual treatment, the social representation of the illness and for persons caught in the web of definitions and practices. The notion of self-infliction continues to be conceptualized as emerging from the essential psychology of the individual, rather than from socially constructed experiences of individuals and their actions. One of the key effects of this notion of self-inflicted illness is that it continues to position individuals as subjects of their own pathology and over which they have little control.

The period between 1930 and 1950 is typified by the rising scientific underpinning of psychiatric practices. It was also a period in which the professionalization of psychiatrists was highly organized and integrated into a broader and systematic regulation of insanity. This system was enforced through the interrelationships between psychiatric practice, the passing of legislature that resulted in Mental Health Acts and the penal system. The extent of the diagnosis and treatment of mental illnesses in women was profound, and psychiatric practices provided few opportunities for patients to contribute to either the explanations of their distress or overcoming what were diagnosed as being psychiatric problems. Anorexia nervosa continued to appear in medical and psychiatric literature throughout several decades, and authors emphasized that the diagnosis was specific to women, overwhelmingly young women. Although there were no significant debates about anorexia nervosa during the following decades this situation did not remain unchallenged, and the 1970s brought a resurgence of interest and criticism. In the next chapter I will summarize the early introduction of the social explanation of mental illness that later influenced the resurgence of interest in anorexia nervosa. I also discuss the emergence of these developments and the ways in which various feminist and social theories have remained peripheral to the dominance of the medical approach to anorexia nervosa.

3
Early Social, Cultural and Feminist Theories of Anorexia Nervosa

During the resurgence of interest in anorexia nervosa in the 1970s a new group of authors also wrote about the condition. The experts who wrote about anorexia nervosa had become a significantly more diverse group, and the overwhelming prevalence in young women was a key concern. Scientific medical literature continued to dominate the explanation and treatment of anorexia nervosa through psychiatric practice, but social theorists, psychologists and feminist writers, began to introduce several different theories about the aetiology of anorexia nervosa. Since the turn of the twentieth century anorexia nervosa has been defined as a phenomenon that included a residual psychopathological aetiology. Of these new writings, feminist theories of anorexia nervosa included the first major challenge to the medical model. The reason for the re-emergence of anorexia nervosa, feminist writers argued, was because it was a form of female social protest (Orbach, 1978, 1986). This explanation linked the appearance of anorexia nervosa during the late nineteenth and twentieth centuries with the emergence of feminist campaigns that challenged the social, political and economic inequalities between women and men.

In this chapter I describe the development and diversification of theories of anorexia nervosa through the 1970s and up to the late 1980s. I will examine three main themes in academic writings that increasingly emphasized the social and cultural dimensions of psychological problems in the explanations of anorexia nervosa. The first theme focuses on the growing disenchantment with psychiatry that was evident in Europe and America during the mid-twentieth century onwards. The second theme describes the developing psychoanalytic movement of the 1960s onwards, the use of Freud's work, neo-Freudian theories, and examines how social relationships within families were linked with the onset of anorexia nervosa. In the third theme I explore the early feminist contributions to the explanation of anorexia nervosa. These feminist writings are of considerable importance because they introduced a conceptualization of anorexia nervosa that drew directly on women's experiences of themselves and social relationships. In particular, feminist writers articulated the interrelationships between women's experiences of living in Western societies, the effects of a subordinate social position and the denial of food by women.

The growing disenchantment with psychiatry

During the 1960s a growing number of therapists, academics and researchers argued that mental illness was intrinsically related to the social conditions of an individual's life and that the notion of an underlying disease causation was neither capable of being proven nor desirable in terms of developing effective treatments. The diversification of theories about the origins of mental illness began to take a social turn related to the changing social and political conditions also occurring in Britain and America during this period. There were many streams of thought that contributed to the social turn in the explanation of mental illness. I briefly summarize only a few of the key writers who became associated with critiques of psychiatry, dubbed the anti-psychiatry movement, and how they introduced social explanations. This summary provides a context for understanding how this social turn was later used to explain anorexia nervosa.

R.D. Laing was a major proponent of the social origins of schizophrenia. Laing co-authored with Esterson a book entitled *Sanity, Madness and the Family* in 1964 and was the first major consideration of the family and its role in the onset of psychological disturbance. In this book the authors argued that families, particularly parents' relationships, created patterns of dysfunctional behaviours in family members through inconsistent and contradictory actions. Laing and Esterson interpreted what they observed in these families using a framework of existential philosophy, and recovery from schizophrenia involved facilitating patients through an intricate passage of self-discovery.

Thomas Szasz (1971, 1972), an American libertarian, went further in his radical examination of psychiatry as a political ideology. Szasz casts modern forms of psychiatric practices as camouflaging the moral dimensions of human behaviours. In his critical appraisals of psychiatry there are numerous insights into the strategic effects of the political organization of madness, underlying these writings is the quest to recognize the moral responsibility of individual actions and make decisions based on this premise rather than those promulgated by psychiatry.

Erving Goffman's (1968) ethnographic analysis of total institutions, *Asylums*, first published in 1961, gives a compelling account of the lives of the inpatients of St Elizabeth's Psychiatric Hospital, Washington, DC. Goffman described the processes that were part of the taken-for-granted world of the psychiatric staff during 1955–6, but which for the patients introduced a series of dehumanizing and humiliating practices that depersonalized them and constructed their 'non-identities'. These processes served various functions for the psychiatrist and encouraged patient compliance with institutional regimes.

These critiques of psychiatry included a focus on therapeutic alternatives to invasive procedures. The foundation of the Arbours Association in London by Dr Morton Schatzman, Vivien Millett, Roberta and Joseph Berke, is an example of an attempt to restructure therapy for mental illness.

The Association established several therapeutic communities based on a philosophy that encouraged respectfulness between its residents and residents' participation in the running and workings of the community. While this approach was not entirely successful with all its residents, the majority had significantly improved their emotional lives and returned to their homes.

Feminist criticism of psychiatric procedures

Feminist criticism was beginning to grow during the 1970s and challenge the overrepresentation and treatment of women as psychiatric patients. Showalter (1987) writes about traditional psychiatric treatments such as ECT in a compelling account of their overuse with women patients. This work also draws attention to the concerns and disquiet that have surrounded the use of these treatments for many decades.

> Although serious questions have been raised about the effectiveness and the ethics of all three (treatments), none has been completely discredited, and all are still in active, if diminished, use today. (Showalter, 1987: 205)

There is no doubt that these treatments were also applied to women diagnosed with anorexia nervosa. The use of electroconvulsive therapy as a treatment for prolonged anorexia has continued over the course of several decades. In a paper entitled 'The use of electroconvulsive therapy in patients with intractable anorexia nervosa' published by Ferguson (1993), three cases are presented with a 'positive response' to ECT reported in two out of three patients. Despite its findings indicating a positive response the paper does not provide evidence in support of the use of ECT with anorexia nervosa for two reasons. First, the author does not compare the treatment outcomes with other treatments for anorexia nervosa. Second, the author uses a narrow definition of what 'successful use' constitutes which includes only the measurement of patients' weight gain. The criteria for a 'positive response' in this review is overwhelmingly defined by the maintenance of weight gain, despite the fact that in one case the woman had begun heavily drinking alcohol, remained seclusive and did not resume work. The extent to which electroconvulsive therapy is used to treat anorexia nervosa is difficult to determine accurately because it is more commonly used in the treatment of chronic depression. There are numerous complexities surrounding co-morbidity, particularly the diagnosis of depression and anorexia nervosa that make it problematic to assume that all recorded treatments of depression do not include some cases of anorexia nervosa.

Bertagnoli and Borchardt's (1990) review of the use of electroconvulsive therapy with children and adolescents diagnosed with bipolar disorder and depression indicates there are too few studies to make a judgement of its use with anorexia nervosa. This paper presents two cases that are defined solely in terms of the psychiatric categorization of patients' behaviour. There is no mention of the social conditions of the patients' lives, the family relationships preceding the patients' psychiatric symptoms, or investigation of the possibility that the young women had undergone some form of psychological trauma from an external event. In the subsequent catalogue of studies of the use of ECT children and adolescents are overwhelmingly regarded as being treated for schizophrenic, depressive or bipolar disorders. All these examples fail to locate the assessment of individuals within a comprehensive framework, and particularly exclude the social and systemic dimensions of a person's life.

Social aspects of anorexia nervosa and Freud's writings

Discussion of the social aspects of mental illness also developed alongside the family therapy movement and family systems theory, which, in part, built upon the work of Laing and Esterson (1964). Family therapy approached the treatment of psychological problems differently, involving the family, rather than the individual, as the object of therapy and change. Common to many of the emerging theories of the social aspects of mental illness was the increasing criticism of the family, and this was also the case in the diversification of theories about anorexia nervosa. To some extent, as we shall see in the next section, this critique attempted to shift the emphasis away from the individual towards problems of the Western nuclear family. The significance of Freud's writings runs through many of these psychiatric views. I will now turn to some specific examples of the explanation of social factors and anorexia nervosa and discuss the extent to which Freud's work continued to link the refusal to eat with the notion of an underlying psychopathology.

Psychoanalytic theories of the socio-cultural dimension of anorexia nervosa

Freud and neo-Freudian ideas related to food refusal

Freud's writings about the family and psychosexual development have been most influential for the explanation of anorexia nervosa. In the *Introductory Lectures on Psychoanalysis (1915–17)* Freud (1973) argued that family relationships were based on sexual complexes, and the nature of family dynamics had significant implications for the psychosexual development of individual personality and emotional states. Underlying family dynamics and psychosexual development was Freud's biological instinct theory of human development, and together these formed one of his key hypotheses about food refusal. Though, Freud's writings should be interpreted in relation to his views about femininity to evaluate his interpretation of food refusal.

The influence of Freud's early writings are based on two main themes, the nutritional instinct and hysteria. First, Freud argued that impairment in the nutritional instinct was related to the organism's inability to come to terms with sexual excitation. Several psychoanalytic explanations of anorexia nervosa developed this theme with limited efficacy. Dally and Gomez (1979) argued that a young woman's striving for thinness in anorexia nervosa represented the postponement of womanhood and symbolized the rejection of femininity. The woman's lack of body shape and the cessation of menstrual periods during anorexia nervosa were interpreted as reinforcing her success in prolonging childhood and the repression of her fear of womanhood. Second, Freud argued that hysteria was usually associated with femininity. Hysteria was established as having a psychological origin, and Freud interpreted the refusal to eat as a hysterical symptom in his female clients, many of whom revealed to him that male family members had sexually abused them during childhood. In a controversial argument Freud is considered to have made an explicit decision not to treat these reports of sexual abuse as actual events that caused psychological distress, but wrote about them as fantasies (cf. Masson, 1985). In Freud's lectures on femininity, in the *New Introductory Lectures on Psychoanalysis*, he stated: 'I was driven to recognise in the end that these reports were untrue and so came to understand that hysterical symptoms are derived from fantasies and not from real occurrences' (1973: 154).

Freud's writings exacerbated, if not engendered, the confusion which continues to surround the relationship between sexual abuse, women and psychology. This confusion is largely due to Freud's argument that early sexual experiences were imagined rather than having actually taken place in the lives of women and children. The historical tendency within eating disorders literature to locate causation within psychopathology, rather than, for example, in real occurrences such as sexual abuse, has also contributed to reproducing sexual abuse as an issue that is steeped in taboo. Further to this, MacLeod and Saraga (1988) argue that it is not the act of abuse, such as incest, which is the taboo, but the belief of the victims themselves. Women's accounts continue to be undervalued within some therapeutic models and schools of research, and an extensive examination of the relationship between sexual abuse and eating disorders remains absent. This history continues to shape psychological research vis-à-vis sexual abuse, and engenders great reluctance to investigate its relationship with anorexia and bulimia nervosa.

The long-standing influence of psychoanalytic theory in the examination of femininity individualizes anorexia nervosa in a similar way to the discourse of the family. The problem of anorexia nervosa becomes located in the woman's attitude towards sexuality, reducing the analysis to a dichotomy about the rejection/acceptance of heterosexual femininity. This course of thinking is overwhelmingly based on traditional theories about unresolved conflict during psychosexual development. Women's ideas about sexuality are excluded, and non-normative sexualities, such as bisexuality and lesbianism, are utterly pathologized, reproducing a normative discourse about sexuality, women and relationships within the family and broader society.

Following Freud's initial writings a multitude of psychoanalysts reinterpreted his work. Some of these writers made considerable breaks with early Freudian theory and some, such as neo-Freudians Erik Fromm, Karen Horney, Erik Erikson and Melanie Klein, developed selected aspects of Freud's theory of psychosexual development. Erik Erikson is a particular example of how the social turn in psychoanalysis attempted to integrate social relationships into theories of human psychosexual development. The social relationships within the family are a key focus for Erikson's developing theories of childhood ego and identity. This movement also paved the way for the later research on patterns of family interactions and their influence on the psychological development of young women diagnosed with anorexia nervosa.

Family systems theory was developing through the 1970s and Salvador Minuchin was one of the earliest theorists to carry out research involving the observation of young women diagnosed with anorexia nervosa within the context of familial interactional patterns. Minuchin et al. (1978) documented the complex interactional patterns involved during meal times in the homes of women diagnosed with anorexia nervosa and the functions that food refusal served in maintaining these interactions. Furthermore, the Milan School of systemic therapy, particularly the work of Selvini-Palazzoli (1974), developed new therapeutic approaches to anorexia nervosa by working with families to examine traditional relationships and their effects.

The most well known psychoanalyst who developed a unique approach to eating disorders, and particularly anorexia nervosa, was Hilde Bruch. Bruch's analysis of anorexia nervosa was broader than previous adaptations of psychoanalytic theory. She stated that the oral component was important but it was only one factor in the aetiology of anorexia nervosa and that there were many other factors that may well precipitate the onset of eating disorders. Bruch (1974) also documented the family dynamics of individuals diagnosed with anorexia nervosa and the tremendous disorganizing effects of the disorder on the family.

The development of research on the family and eating disorders by psychoanalysts and socio-cultural theorists, and as I will discuss later from some feminist writers, commonly focused on the significance of mothers to a much greater extent than fathers. There is a particular trend in the literature about anorexia nervosa that traces factors within the relationship between the person diagnosed with anorexia nervosa and her (or his) mother. The focus on the mother was, to some extent, developed because historically the mother had responsibility for the provision of food in the family household. Although, this focus also drew on other available discourses that depicted the mother as culpable for a range of problems within the family. For example, early work on infant feeding examined maternal emotional hostility as the main precipitating factor in the onset of a child's reluctance to accept nourishment and the subsequent development of 'infantile dwarfism' (Gardner, 1972). The phenomenon of focusing on the mother in the explanation and resolution of psychological and social problems in academic literature and social welfare policy became known as 'mother-blaming'.

Social analyses of anorexia nervosa did not attempt to develop a critique of the family as a patriarchal institution, and the absence of literature about the father is a key point that has generated debate. During the early 1990s there was a vigorous exchange about patriarchy and anorexia nervosa between Jan Horsfall (1991) and Bryan Turner (1990) due to Turner's article about Hilde Bruch. Turner writes about Bruch's work on anorexia nervosa and her focus on the mother and the daughter's sense of low personal autonomy, but is criticized for omitting sociological analysis of the institution of the family or patriarchy. Horsfall's (1991) criticism of Bryan Turner's (1990) article about Hilde Bruch and anorexia nervosa raises the question about fathers:

> scientists and therapists (male and female) may 'naturally' not notice the role of the father in families labelled pathological: a concomitant of such an un-noticeable bias is the awareness of the mother. Thus we had the most terrible of mothers – the schizophrenogenic mother – in the 1950s and interestingly, descriptions attached to her were exactly the same as those Turner gleans from Bruch regarding the mothers of anorexics, that is an 'over-powering, dominant mother involved in an excessively regulated relationship with her daughter' (Turner, 1990: 162). Hence we must acknowledge Hilda Bruch's training in psychiatry – a notably patriarchal profession. And we must ask what equally charming qualities these invisible fathers would manifest should we look for them. (Horsfall, 1991: 233).

Moreover, Horsfall's (1991) work draws attention to the structuring of psychiatric practice that creates the conditions for overlooking the father's role in anorexia nervosa. She raises the question, what, indeed, would the characteristics be of these absent fathers if we deliberately looked for them? In making the point about the missing fathers in the interpretation of psychopathology, Horsfall (1991) also notes that this tendency is not unique to the research on anorexia nervosa, and is common across a range of clinical domains. Social analyses that employed a family discourse and emphasized the mother–daughter relationship contributed to the individualization of anorexia nervosa by bringing wider social forces into the private sphere. While these analyses constructed different foci in relation to food refusal, they did not realize in practice the radical philosophies that had earlier been put forward by either the anti-psychiatry movement or the women's movement.

Media, femininity and anorexia nervosa

Changing cultural trends in female body shape is an obvious explanation of why women strive to be, and remain thin. Artists throughout history have portrayed women in various ways, and Bruch (1974), developing a psycho-analytic explanation of femininity, strongly argued that these changing representations contributed to the onset of eating disorders. Historical depictions of women included a symbolic preference for pregnant abdomens, large breasts, heavy hips and thighs that continued until the late nineteenth century (Bruch, 1974). Thinness and fragility became feminine attributes of the middle classes of the late nineteenth century. During the late 1960s and early 1970s the rise in mass media created a representation of the ideal feminine body as one that was characterized by thinness. For example, high profile clothing models, such as 'Twiggy', became part of popular culture, and women were positioned to reproduce these cultural icons of femininity. These cultural developments were fundamental to the socio-cultural explanation of the onset of anorexia nervosa (Wooley and Wooley, 1982).

A vast, multi-million dollar 'slimming industry' reinforced the culture of thinness by encouraging practices of 'calorie-counting', 'weight-watching', and 'dieting', so that women could regulate their body size. Calorimetry, which developed at the turn of the century, and used to identify the exogenous nature of obesity (Bruch, 1974), was incorporated into popular magazine diets. 'Slimmers' on 'calorie-controlled diets', in some instances, would repeatedly calculate their daily intakes of food and drink in terms of a specified calorie allowance. Slimming food supplements became commonly used as a means to weight loss during the 1980s, yet, media reports warned consumers about the dangers associated with their usage. *The Guardian*, in an article entitled, 'Slimming aid can boost appetite' in 1986, reported that stimulants contained within slimming supplements increased individual consumption of sucrose and decreased control over appetite leading to disorganized eating behaviour.

Newspaper, magazine and television articles regularly featured celebrities who were suspected to be 'starving' or 'bingeing'. Some of the early reports included Jane Fonda, who 'admitted to having an eating problem', and was a story that received massive media coverage in the 1980s, juxtaposed with a portrayal of her as one of America's 'keep-fit queens'. The biggest attraction about an episode of a British television chat show called *Wogan* was the interviewer asking popular singer Kylie Minogue whether she was anorexic. In addition, women's magazines featured weekly stories about eating disorders. Princess Diana's 'long battle with bulimia' was a common example of the 1980s tabloid interest, and articles attracted enormous revenue from selling the voyeurism of eating disorders.

Bruch's (1978) argument strongly associated cultural representations of femininity with anorexia nervosa. She began to explicate the different uses of eating behaviours by women, insofar as they articulated women's relationship to femininity, and anorexia nervosa was regarded as a specific condition and psychiatric category from which young women suffered. Moreover, eating disorders, anorexia nervosa and bulimia nervosa, themselves became part of popular culture. Bruch (1978) reported that almost all of her clients had heard of anorexia nervosa and were familiar with literature on anorexia nervosa, and suggested that this familiarity may decrease its use as a breakthrough in self-control and imagination.

Social analyses, psychopathology and anorexia nervosa

Social analyses of anorexia nervosa were the first attempts to change the explanation of aetiology from one that was defined solely in terms of psychopathology. Yet, social analyses, unlike feminist perspectives, did not attempt to make an explicit break with medical explanations. Social analyses employed various discourses in the explanation of women and food refusal, including psychoanalytic theory, identity, family dynamics and body image, and expanded psychomedical explanations. These analyses formed both academic and popular contexts for the further development of social analysis within feminist perspectives that later became the first significant contestations of the psychiatric explanation of anorexia nervosa and women. The application of versions of psychoanalytic theory is particularly prevalent in social analyses of anorexia nervosa. The influence of Freud's nineteenth century work on hysteria, which had been crucial to the continued documentation of anorexia nervosa as a nervous disorder, was fundamental to some interpretations. The analysis of family dynamics and psychosexual development was of particular importance to research on anorexia nervosa during the 1960s and 1970s. However, the use of psychoanalytic theory in social analysis continued to individualize the nature of anorexia nervosa rather than comprehensively analyse social aspects. Social explanations during this period did not significantly reconceptualize the aetiology of anorexia nervosa; rather, social dimensions became accepted as 'influences' or 'factors' in psychopathology and subsumed within psychiatric discourse.

The reluctance to seriously support social approaches are related to epistemological differences within the human sciences and to the historical absence of a social theorization of the relationships between social and cultural practices and individual psychology. However, there is no longer an absence of the articulation of social contexts, their relationship to psychology and anorexia nervosa, with explanations drawing on constructivist and social constructionist philosophical movements in psychology (cf. Hepworth, 1994; Hepworth and Griffin, 1990, 1995; White and Epston, 1990). These disciplinary differences continue based on contests over the rigour of explanatory models of psychology. Yet, many social analyses of anorexia nervosa are underpinned by its status as a psychiatric category thus creating a reductionist framework of explanation. This interpretation limits the possibilities to articulate social and cultural aspects by collapsing the complexity and diversity of social practices into pre-existing explanatory frameworks. Consequently, socio-cultural analyses, while expanding the range of social theories of anorexia nervosa, received criticism for not demonstrating clear scientific links with its onset and duration and were regarded inferior to theories constructed through biomedical hypotheses.

Social analyses were also significant in contributing to the context in which early feminist analyses of anorexia nervosa emerged. The introduction of the idea that social factors could be possible causes of anorexia nervosa and the attempts to rethink the role of psychomedical factors in relation to social explanations became key foci of feminist analyses. The particular contribution that social analyses of anorexia nervosa made was introducing various social dimensions, external to the individual, as being possible aetiologies, and this had similarities with the emerging debate about the relationship between women's social oppression and mental health.

Early feminist contributions to the explanation of anorexia nervosa

During the late 1970s and early 1980s resurgence of interest in eating disorders, and particularly anorexia nervosa, feminist writers drew attention to the distress that women experienced in relation to eating and psychological health. Feminist writings proposed several explanations of the links between psychological distress and the social, cultural and political conditions of women. I discuss these explanations in more detail by examining three feminist texts that are examples of key writings of this period.

Three key feminist texts on anorexia nervosa

Susie Orbach's *Hunger Strike* (1986), Kim Chernin's *The Hungry Self* (1986) and Sheila MacLeod's *The Art of Starvation* (1981) put forward three different feminist perspectives on anorexia nervosa; socio-cultural analysis and patriarchal relations; psychoanalytic theories; and existentialism. Feminist theories stood in contrast to medical and psychiatric explanations of anorexia nervosa because of their broad focus on social, familial and political aspects of women's lives. Feminist analyses attempted to depart, in varying degrees, from the dominant medical approach to anorexia nervosa arguing that the medical paradigm limited rather than facilitated recovery from anorexia nervosa. Medical processes were criticized for their narrow definition of women's experiences and contribution to the control of women's behaviours. In the following sections I discuss the extent to which these early feminist writings achieved a reconceptualization of anorexia nervosa.

Feminist writings brought the voice of women who refused food to the fore, and, in some cases, women who had been diagnosed with anorexia nervosa, such as Sheila MacLeod, were the authors of these books. However, there were ideological and theoretical difficulties with feminist analyses of anorexia nervosa. While social structure was recognized as being significant in women's experiences, the use of categories, such as anorexia nervosa and the influence of psychoanalytic theory, both based on exclusively historical patriarchal definitions of women, continued to be present in these analyses. The use of psychoanalytic approaches by feminists and their relationship within feminist therapies is a continuing focus of debate (cf. Burman, 1992; Mitchell, 1975; Sayers, 1986). While key feminist psychoanalytic texts on anorexia nervosa are discussed I do not provide a detailed examination of the issues that feminists have debated in using Freud's writings. Though, I argue that psychoanalytic based feminist analysis contributed to the failure to establish the shift away from a psychomedical epistemology about women and anorexia nervosa, which had been so much a part of their initial promise.

The centrality of the mother–daughter relationship in feminist analyses of the family

Freudian theory had been used in the literature on eating disorders by drawing specifically on the significance that the oral component had in relation to unresolved Electra conflict. In doing so psychoanalytic writers tended to overemphasize the importance of 'oral impregnation' as being symbolic of the woman's fear of femininity in anorexia nervosa. Although feminist psychoanalysts began to shift the focus away from 'oral impregnation theory' towards a discourse of the family, this often meant an examination of the mother–daughter relationship, but not the father–daughter relationship. The exclusion of the father in literature on anorexia nervosa was introduced earlier in the chapter; Lawrence (1984) reinforces this point by noting that often the word 'family' is equated with 'mother'. The representation of mothers as the providers of nurturance, and an assumed naturally defined maternal role, positioned women as the bedrock of domestic life. There may well be a 'special' relationship between a mother and a daughter, but the articulation of this relationship within feminist texts was limited as an explanation for anorexia nervosa, depicting these women as struggling because of problems and difficulties. Lawrence states: 'I can say with certainty that I have never worked with an anorexic woman who had a straight-forward relationship with her mother' (1984: 67). Lawrence (1984) does not, here, go on to discuss what was meant by a 'straight-forward' relationship between the mother and daughter.

Chernin (1986), like other feminist writers in the 1980s, examined socio-cultural identity and women. Using a Kleinian perspective, she illustrated how the separation between mother and daughter is made more difficult by women's ambiguous social role which the daughter is unprepared to take on. Anorexia nervosa became a vehicle through which the daughter could return to her mother and recapture the safety of the mother–daughter bond. The reported difficulties for anorexics surround issues of separateness and differentiation (Lawrence, 1984), and as a result of these feelings an anorexic constructs a regressive relationship with her mother. In addition to this Bruch (1974) argued that the anorexic's home was often 'too good' because her mother often anticipated her daughter's needs. Such 'meticulous care', Bruch (1974) stated, led to the development of dysfunctional feeding practices and the child's self-awareness of hunger and satiation did not fully develop. The mother's anticipation created a situation whereby self-worth and independence were not developed and presented difficulties for the child, particularly during adolescence when those skills were required (Bruch, 1974; Winnicott, 1964).

Lawrence (1984) described the situation in which the parents of an anorexic found themselves. She stated that for parents the anorexic person was often seen as a 'terrifying transformation', which was made even more frightening by an accompanying personality change. Often the family of an anorexic came to accept a new way of life where they were in constant fear of their daughter's actions. All the family members became sensitive to this 'perceived tyranny' which they could become tired of and even come to despise. For these reasons Lawrence (1984) argued that the family should receive a certain amount of sympathy owing to the suffering it, too, endures while living so closely with an anorexic.

The family structure was not fully examined in feminist analyses, rather family relationships, specifically the mother–daughter relationship, were the key focus. The concept of a developing childhood identity involving the same-sex parent made mothers a fundamental link in the explanation of psychology, identification processes and the onset of anorexia nervosa. The use of frameworks of identity as explanations of anorexia nervosa is discussed in more detail in Chapter 4. A young woman is positioned vis-à-vis an identification process with her mother, through which it is assumed she achieves, or not, sexual differentiation. Therefore, young women who become diagnosed with anorexia nervosa are understood as struggling with the separation of their mothers' identity from their own, or, alternatively, that they experience role confusion between their mother's life and their own.

> the essentially ambivalent nature of the mother–daughter relationship, and the understanding of how the social requirement that women must emotionally service and address the needs of others is expressed in the way in which the relating proceeds in the early mother–daughter relationship. (Orbach, 1986: 162)

Orbach believed that the mother–daughter relationship should be explored during therapy, particularly the way it taught the daughter how to feel about herself and relate to others. In short, the relationship was understood as a model for the daughter to identify with, and one that was constitutive of her future relationships. Women became used to not expressing their own needs and felt ashamed and guilty when they did, and so anorexia nervosa, understood in this way, was an extension of women's denial of the need for nourishment. Writers argued that the denial of basic needs was a familiar experience for women and intrinsically linked with the development of identity. Further to this, Orbach argued that the co-existence of love and hate was fundamental to the daughter's self-regard, and this dialectic became transferred to the unconscious meanings that women were thought to attach to food.

Chernin examined the mother–daughter relationship as one that was problematic because of conflict about separation and differentiation. The difficulties arose from the daughter's increasing awareness of her mother's life of subordination, which in turn encouraged a sense of guilt in the daughter. Chernin wrote:

> This anguished concern about the mother is hidden just beneath the surface of the eating problem. (1986: 43)

Imagine a woman stepping out joyfully into her own new life who now feels herself torn between her loyalty to her mother and her response to that new woman, that new female being we are all struggling toward. (1986: 45)

This guilt was exacerbated because the mother and daughter experienced a shared identity as women, but the daughter was developing her own life during a period when women's roles are changing, and where multiple roles exist. MacLeod wrote: 'to the anorexic, the most important member of that family is her mother' (1981: 132).

MacLeod included the mother–daughter relationship as being influential in the development of anorexia nervosa. Like Orbach (1986), MacLeod (1981) suggested that a certain ambivalence surrounded this relationship that could later manifest in what she described as being a deprived existential state of anorexia nervosa. The deprivation within the mother–daughter bond was argued to be representative of the starvation of 'mother-love'. MacLeod's explanation of anorexia nervosa differed from Chernin in that she argued that the ambivalence that surrounded the relationship was fundamental to the development of the anorexic state. The experience of ambivalence became embedded in the very way women experience 'being-in-the-world'. Similarly, Orbach argued that the mother's ambivalence towards her daughter taught the daughter how to feel about herself.

All three texts focused on the mother and how she was related to the development of anorexia nervosa to the complete exclusion of the father. This exclusion had particular consequences for the development of explanations of anorexia nervosa because feminists, particularly feminist psychoanalysts, did not address the issue of sexual abuse. Until the late 1980s, when research at the Women's Therapy Centre began to address sexual violence and its relation to eating disorders, the role of male family members has been absent (cf. Sayers, 1988). Explanations of anorexia nervosa using a discourse of the family have described how maternal relations define women's psychological development. Further to this, Orbach (1986) described how in caring for a woman with anorexia nervosa, women themselves experienced their unmet needs. As adults, she argued, women were encouraged to repress closeness with other women – an experience which had been part of their lives for many years, while men could replace that love with 'wives' and 'lovers'.

Anorexia nervosa as a problem of identity in feminist texts

In all three texts (Chernin, 1986; MacLeod, 1981; Orbach, 1986) the problem of identity was discussed as a key site for the interpretation of anorexia nervosa. In part, the notion of identity drew on a field of research that analysed sex role expectations, in which role conflict was understood as being internalized rather than translated into social action. Consequently, an anorexic's identity was problematic and to be grappled with either in isolation, or in terms of the feminine identity that she was assumed to share with her mother. Orbach argued that the confusing social identity of women in contemporary society was pivotal in producing anorexic women: 'The anorexic's refusal to accept her culturally defined role is seen to be per se pathological, not an extremely complicated response to a confusing social identity' (1986: 25). Women had to try and make sense of the confusing expectations of them, and anorexia nervosa was a manifestation of the oppressive nature of that position. Orbach argued that amid the confusion that surrounded the dual roles of women – motherhood and having a career – women attempt to regain control over their lives through anorexia nervosa. Women took control of their own bodies by denying themselves food.

Chernin (1986) argued that identity development was a crucial issue that needed to be explored in consultations with women who had eating disorders. Women's relationship to food, Chernin argued, could be traced to the complexity that surrounds the mother–daughter relationship, and the daughter's realization of transcending her mother's experiences:

> They are lost, empty, restless, confused and dissatisfied. They are struggling with all the questions of identity their mothers also faced. (1986: 20–1)

> Eating disorders express our uncertainties, our buried anguish, our unconfessed confusion of identity. (1986: 36)

The daughter faced the task of developing her own identity in a society that held diverse expectations of women. Together with this, the daughter's identification with her mother involved issues about transcending her mother's life because of her different experiences of social expectations.

Alternatively, for MacLeod identity was something to be 'fought' for: 'Anorexia nervosa is fundamentally about an identity crisis' (1981: 64).

Anorexia represented a crisis about women's personal existence based on the lack of women's autonomy to develop an 'authentic' identity. In this sense, anorexia nervosa was a woman's rebellion against her experiences of subordination. The anorexic woman was represented as fighting for an existence whereby she could develop an identity as a person. The resolution of the 'identity crisis' is regarded as being essential for recovery, but because anorexia nervosa was seen as a disease, and since it was located within individual women, they are required to change rather than society. Henriques et al. (1984) argue that the notion of identity individualizes women's oppression and resistance. This process of individualization is exemplified in texts about anorexia nervosa.

Anorexia nervosa and the anorexic: the object and subject of discourse

One of the ways in which feminist texts reproduced explanations of anorexia nervosa rather than creating a break with existing theories was through their use of medical language. In the next sections the use of the category anorexia nervosa is discussed, and argued to have contributed to the reproduction of the object of discourse, anorexia nervosa, as a psychiatric category. Reference to women as 'anorexics' is an effect of this discourse and argued to reproduce the position of women as subjects within that discourse.

Hunger Strike *by Susie Orbach (1986)*   The historical origins of anorexia nervosa were mentioned in Orbach's (1986) text, yet she concluded: '(anorexia) has now come into popular and technical use so widely that a more accurate term seems unlikely to be adopted' (Orbach, 1986: 48). Orbach recognized the problematic nature of the term anorexia nervosa, but continued to employ the term to represent her argument although that argument was constructed through a very different epistemology. Feminist analyses aimed to challenge the acceptance of terminology through which explanations of women were developed, and particularly on the basis that specific explanations of psychological phenomenon had been written exclusively by male physicians. However, Orbach did clarify her use of the term: 'I use anorexia in its broadest possible sense to describe those women who are invested in not eating and have become scared of food and what it can do to them' (1986: 13).

The Hungry Self *by Kim Chernin (1986)*   Chernin's text discussed women and eating disorders using, amongst others, a Kleinian (1959) psychoanalytic perspective that is based on object–relations theory. Chernin described how there may be specific conflicts that underlie eating disorders and drew on the works of psychoanalytic theorists Freud, Erikson and Klein. She included a personal narrative where she relates her own experience of eating disorders, as well as describing consultations with women who had been diagnosed as having an eating disorder. Both anorexia nervosa and bulimia nervosa are discussed in this text, but here only the use of the term anorexia nervosa is discussed, though it often appears abbreviated as just anorexia, for example: 'The *New York Times*, on July 14, 1982, reported that anorexia afflicts 1 in 250 girls between 16 and 18 years of age' Other estimates run as high as 1 in 100. Since less than 8 per cent of all anorexics are male, we are forced to conclude that, in our time, eating disorders are a distinct form of female suffering. (Chernin, 1986: 13). In her discussion of women diagnosed as 'anorectic' she includes the singer Karen Carpenter 'who died of a heart attack at the age of thirty-two, in a state of depletion caused by years of suffering from anorexia and bulimia' (Chernin, 1986: 12).

   These texts exemplify the acceptance (again with some reservations) of the term anorexia as representing a definable condition. Karen Carpenter's death was described as being caused by anorexia and bulimia. Chernin used the term without questioning its meaning or utility. Her analysis, like other feminist texts, attempted to forge alternative interpretations of eating disorders, but the use of the term remained uncritical of the medical documentation of anorexia nervosa.

The Art of Starvation *by Sheila MacLeod (1981)*   MacLeod drew broadly on an existential approach to anorexia nervosa. Female identity was articulated as being central to the state of anorexia. Anorexia was seen as being a manifestation of an existential crisis resulting from confusion experienced about 'being-in-the-world'. MacLeod's text was also largely based on a narrative of herself developing anorexia nervosa throughout adolescence and adulthood. In common with both Orbach (1986) and Chernin (1986), MacLeod emphasized that female identity in contemporary society is an area that is fraught with difficulties and obstacles. For Orbach (1986) the roots of that confusion resided in female oppression, but Chernin (1986) located it within the unconscious conflict of the mother–daughter relationship. MacLeod's analysis put forward a different view that attempted to articulate the complexity of the relationship between social factors and individual psyche, for example: 'In my experience, anorexia nervosa is not a matter of slimming which has somehow or other got out of hand' (1981: 10).

Anorexia nervosa, emerging through a dominant epistemological structure, also constructed subject positions for women who refused food: 'anorectics', which were later reproduced through feminist writings. For example, Orbach wrote: 'When a therapist first meets an anorectic woman, she cannot help but be aware of several striking physical features' (1986: 181). In contrast to this Orbach (1986) argued that the classification of a group of women on the basis of anorexia nervosa encouraged a certain way of thinking about women, such as, that they have a mystique, or are vulnerable to work with when they are very low weight. This argument recognized the effects of being seen as anorexic but did not challenge the historical, political and social contexts through which this had come about. Furthermore, this positioning of women had implications for feminist therapy and specifically the client–therapist relationship but were not addressed. Similarly, Chernin described women as anorectic: 'Anorectic women are frequently described by their parents and siblings ... in terms that explicitly evoke the concentration camp experience.' (1986: 60).

Reference to women as anorexics had an effect of immediately separating them from other women. The term divided women into groups of those who were anorexic and those who were not. Interestingly, Orbach positioned herself as author in her work *Hunger Strike* (1986), whereas Chernin and MacLeod positioned themselves as anorexic women or recovered anorexics. Like Orbach (1986) and Chernin (1986), MacLeod described women who refuse food as anorexics. MacLeod wrote: 'My experience shows that getting the anorexic to eat is only half the battle' (1981: 122).

MacLeod offered an interesting analysis because it provided an insight into the meaning of anorexia for a woman in terms of everyday living. Anorexia nervosa from an existential perspective became a symbol of oppression, and simultaneously, also a symbol of resistance. The anorexic for MacLeod was a woman who had achieved a sense of freedom from the boundaries of an oppressed life. MacLeod (1981: 83) stated, 'I was free at last!', as a description of her own feelings on becoming a 'successful anorexic'. This kind of existence involved an aesthetic element, one which had also been associated with women throughout history, but was always impossible to attain. It was a form of aestheticism that was based on a dialectic of perfectionism. MacLeod drawing on this discourse argued that: 'Anorexic's, being perfectionists, prefer to do things properly or not at all' (1981: 129).

MacLeod's central thesis was that starvation is an art, and is an art with which women become overwhelmingly preoccupied and that takes place within the psychological realm: 'The psychological realm, where alone I believed myself to exist' (1981: 96). What was different about MacLeod's text was the importance that she attached to women's subjectivity, and breadth of experiences, whereas so much previous work, both medical and feminist, had focused on the anorexic's preoccupation with body size.

Feminist praxis: Orbach and the Women's Therapy Centre

Orbach's (1978) *Fat is a Feminist Issue* became overwhelmingly influential amid the expanding feminist literature on 'eating disorders'. Orbach's theory about compulsive eating argued that emotional upheaval or deprivation would lead to 'comfort-eating'; that carbohydrates could satisfy an emotional hunger. Orbach, a co-founder with Marilyn Lawrence, of the Women's Therapy Centre (WTC) in London, published *Hunger Strike* in 1986 which further elaborated a feminist voice about the aetiology of anorexia nervosa. Feminist psychotherapist's at the Women's Therapy Centre argued that there was an intrinsic link between eating disorders and patriarchal society (Lawrence and Lowenstein, 1979; Orbach, 1986). Some of the early counter-practices to medical treatments for anorexia nervosa were to be found in Orbach and Lawrence's therapy groups and workshops that were held at the WTC. This forum supported sufferers to develop their understandings of the problematic relationships between women and food and aimed to overcome difficulties through an exploration of their social position.

The concept of socialization was a major factor in this examination. The role of women in contemporary society was analysed using what can be broadly defined as feminist psychoanalytic theory. Simply put, this theory argued that the socialization of female children in Western societies encouraged women to attach unconscious meanings to food. These meanings included feelings of guilt, the practice of comfort-eating and self-denial of nutritional needs, and their manifestations as eating disorders became expressions of women's exploitation in a patriarchal culture (Orbach, 1986). Additionally, increasing consumerism used women to advertise commodities by positioning them alongside desirable objects, and in doing so women also became advertised as objects of desire. This commodification alienated women from themselves, reinforced their inferior social status, and encouraged a culture of self-evaluation in terms of physical appearance.

Anorexia, Orbach (1986) argued, became a 'metaphor for our age' because it became a response to a confusing social identity that women continually experienced. Orbach wrote: 'all women live with a tension about their place in the World' (1986: 29). Orbach draws on the argument that there is a dominant ideology that equates sexual attractiveness with slimness. This ideology is understood as being further reinforced through male heterosexual socialized preferences to view women who are slim as being attractive. Leon (1980) commented that it was particularly sad that throughout childhood and adolescence girls are encouraged to define themselves in terms of their appearance and this is then carried through to later life. She argued that socialization processes were significant aetiological factors and that it was only by moving away from these processes that the incidence of conditions such as anorexia nervosa would be decreased. Orbach, together with other feminist therapists at the WTC, developed a feminist approach that included both psychoanalysis and criticism of social structure. There-fore, even though the conceptualization of women's refusal to eat was related to social positions, the treatment focus for women was to challenge expressions of unconscious meanings within themselves.

Feminist analyses of anorexia nervosa presented several new approaches to the explanation of women and food. Kim Chernin and Sheila MacLeod spoke about their personal experiences of anorexia nervosa as well as con-tributing to the diversification of the range of alternative perspectives on eating disorders. Moreover, this process demonstrated the serious intention and value of women defining their own reasons for their actions. It would appear that there was a break with the historical medical legacy that had dominated the management of women who refused food since the last century. However, in the early feminist texts of the 1980s there were a number of problems with feminist ideology and individual analytical per-spectives. Orbach (1986) had focused on the consequences that patriarchal societies had for women and the limits and contradictions of the female 'role', but excluded any detailed analysis of the 'role' of men in those societies. The feminist socio-cultural approach was successful in articulat-ing the need to examine society in relation to anorexia nervosa and the introduction of sexual politics, but was limited in its explication of how specific social, cultural and ideological conditions reproduced patriarchal societies and constructed subject positions for women.

The main issue for Chernin (1986) had been the analysis of eating disorders within the mother–daughter relationship and the consequences that this had for the development of female identity. While this relationship is undoubtedly important because of the commonality of gender experi-ences, the exclusive focus on this relationship as if it were a precursor to the onset of anorexia nervosa was problematic. The analytical frame of the mother–daughter relationship involved a sense of blaming the mother for her daughter's eating difficulties. Even though Chernin's approach was not one that apportioned blame, it was a consequence of the process of examin-ing individual psychology and roles in isolation from the socio-cultural con-ditions through which they were constructed.

MacLeod (1981), in attributing anorexia nervosa to women's existential crises involved ambiguities in relation to the reconciliation of feminist and existentialist theories. Her analysis began with the development of an inte-grated feminist/existential perspective on anorexia. However, she made it explicit that she doubted that the 'ruling ideology' should be feminist in understanding anorexics. Existentialism in MacLeod's work was introduced more as a possible source for the interpretation of anorexia nervosa rather than as a detailed explication of an existentialist position vis-à-vis the range of issues related to women, feminism and food.

The individualization of women and food refusal was common to all three perspectives with interpretations drawing on constructs of psychoanalytic theory, social role theory or the 'self', within the humanist paradigm that separated individual psychology from social processes. The use of this philosophical framework had two main consequences for the treatment of women. First, a woman was seen as needing to be 'cured' from the condition known as anorexia nervosa, a direct recourse to the medical model. Second, the process of change was located within individual women rather than through social practices.

Reproduction of the medical and psychiatric discourses of anorexia nervosa

Anorexia nervosa had been constructed through medical discourses during the late nineteenth century as discussed in Chapter 2. The reproduction of medical and psychiatric discourses in early feminist texts, especially the writings of Cherin (1984), MacLeod (1981) and Orbach (1986), has developed in three ways. First, through the focus on psychological phenomena related to the mother–daughter relationship. Second, by retaining the use of the category anorexia nervosa. Third, through the effects of language use and the reproduction of the position of women as subjects of dominant discourses about anorexia nervosa.

The focus on the family, specifically the mother–daughter relationship, and identity in all three texts were also problematic because of the particular form of psychoanalytic theory to which feminist writers referred. One of the criticisms of the use of these discourses was that the mother–daughter relationship was examined, and particular features emphasized, to the exclusion of the father's role. Lawrence (1984) argued that very few anorexics were attached to their fathers, while the majority were interested in him, defined by feelings of fear, adoration, loathing and wanting to please. Overwhelmingly, the father–daughter relationship involved issues that related to the daughter's sexual role as an adult. The anorexic was commonly regarded as refusing food in order to slow down adult development and regain dependency on her parents. This analysis oversimplified the father–daughter relationship and wider social norms. The emphasis on the mother–daughter relationship was seen as being significant exactly because of its particular characteristics. A commonly reported characteristic was the young woman diagnosed with anorexia nervosa being overprotective towards her mother. Lawrence (1984) made an interesting distinction between the 'anorexic's' description of her relationship with her mother as one depicted as being 'idyllic', and the mother's description of the relationship as being 'demanding' and 'tiring'. The range of numerous conditions through which the interpretation of the daughter's desire to have a good relationship with her mother was not, therefore, fully explored.

There are numerous interpretations of psychoanalytic theory, and I am not denying that these may have some use in the explanation of anorexia nervosa. Here, though, I am concerned with specific concepts developed by Freud during the late nineteenth century that were used in the conceptualization of anorexia nervosa at the turn of the century and continued in various texts. In particular, Freud's popularization of the notion of hysteria reinforced the representation of the women who refused food as being driven by internal forces, irrational and out of control. Feminist writers have criticized the pathologization of women's actions through referring to them as 'hysterical' behaviour (cf. Showalter, 1987). Yet, it is troubling that the early conceptualization of women and anorexia nervosa, later developed by Freud, drew on similar psychoanalytic theory to that which twentieth century feminist writers used in developing feminist psychoanalytic perspectives on anorexia nervosa. The ideology of femininity that Freudian psychoanalytic theory drew on and reproduced overwhelmingly represented women dominated by psychopathology, and intrinsically linked to their reproductive, sexual and 'irrational' natures (Freud, 1973). The development of feminist writings about anorexia nervosa during the 1980s attempted to challenge the dominant psychomedical model by introducing explanations of women related to social, cultural and political conditions. This movement aimed to dispel the mythology about the peculiarity of the female psyche and women's so-called potentiality to develop 'nervous diseases'. For this reason feminist psychoanalytic perspectives on anorexia nervosa needed to be explicit about their point of departure from traditional Freudian psychoanalysis.

The term anorexia nervosa was employed in all three feminist texts. Orbach (1986) acknowledged the unsatisfactory and inaccurate nature of the term, but there was no attempt to discuss this further. Orbach wrote:

> Anorexia nervosa is perhaps the most dramatic outcome of the culture's obsession with regulating body size. In the last ten years this psychological syndrome has risen to epidemic proportions. (1986: 23)

While feminists had moved away from the nineteenth century conceptions surrounding the organic, moral and psychological causation of anorexia nervosa in favour of versions of socio-cultural analysis, these analyses continued to draw on and reproduced medical hegemony. Earlier, the continued use of the term was argued to reproduce ideological premises through which the medical management of eating disorders was structured and this ideology was inconsistent with the aims of feminist analyses. Yet, the tension between psychomedical and feminist ideologies has not been resolved in relation to anorexia nervosa. There are no alternative references for food refusal and the use of anorexia nervosa is mostly carried out uncritically.

While feminist perspectives on anorexia nervosa developed more qualitatively rich analyses of women and self-starvation, the similarities between antithetical positions, medicine and feminism, demonstrate how modernist epistemology continued to structure the construction of knowledge about women and anorexia nervosa and how discourses function. A series of contradictory positions in feminist literature developed based on the dominance of the medical model of anorexia nervosa. Feminist writers on anorexia nervosa during the 1980s were in a difficult position, and to some extent this difficulty has continued. In one sense feminist explanations of anorexia nervosa have provided significant theoretical insights, but they were constrained by psychomedical discourse. Feminist analyses that employed specific discourses about self-starvation demonstrate how alternative conceptualizations of women who refuse food are structured through historical ideas, and that these ideas constrain the potential for the transformation of practice.

PART II
HEALTH CARE WORKERS' CONSTRUCTIONS OF ANOREXIA NERVOSA

Introduction to the interviews with health care workers

Throughout Part I, I have discussed religious, medical, early social and feminist explanations of self-starvation and anorexia nervosa. For centuries, as this discussion shows, women have been associated with the denial of food, and anorexia nervosa continues to be considered in psychiatric texts as a predominantly female mental illness. Moreover, the discovery of anorexia nervosa within the late nineteenth century was made possible by drawing on a specific discourse of femininity and range of related discourses that were necessary to its construction (Hepworth and Griffin, 1990). In the following chapters I examine the construction of anorexia nervosa in interviews with different health care workers. First, though, it is necessary to summarize briefly the organization, conduct and analysis of the interviews.

The interview analysis differed from the discourse analysis method used in Chapter 2. The analysis of the discovery of anorexia nervosa in Chapter 2 demonstrated how historical, social and institutional ideas and practices secured its definition through five key discourses. This work raised a series of questions that I wanted to ask about anorexia nervosa and more recent practices. I interviewed health care workers because they comprised the main group who worked with dominant ideas about preventing and treating anorexia nervosa. I was interested in the ways in which health care workers constructed anorexia nervosa as a contemporary problem. I developed the interview questions from the key areas that had emerged from the historical analysis of anorexia nervosa and a literature review of current theories of anorexia nervosa. I asked open-ended questions about what constituted anorexia nervosa, its cause, treatment, relationship with gender, identity, therapy and recovery.

I interviewed eleven health care workers, including two general practitioners, two psychiatrists, three clinical psychologists, three psychiatric nurses and one feminist therapist. These professional groups were selected because they represented the diverse range of therapists to which a person diagnosed with anorexia nervosa could be referred. They all had experience in treating anorexic patients and had current responsibilities, relative to their professional roles, for the diagnosis and treatment and/or day-to-day care of these patients at the time the interviews were conducted. There were four male interviewees (one general practitioner, one psychiatrist and two clinical psychologists) and seven females (one general practitioner, one psychiatrist, one clinical psychologist, three psychiatric nurses and one feminist therapist). The general practitioners, psychiatrists, clinical psychologists and psychiatric nurses worked within the same National Health Service (NHS) area of England, UK, and, therefore, worked with similar health care resources and referral routes for anorexia nervosa.

The interviews took place in general practitioner surgeries, the district psychology service headquarters for the NHS region, a psychiatric hospital and the Women's Therapy Centre, London. The organization of these interviews was complicated by the nature of the practitioners' work and on several occasions interviewees were not available for their arranged interviews because of emergency calls, yet made other times to be interviewed. In addition to this other health care workers were reluctant to be interviewed because of the lack of time they had. Those who did agree to be interviewed in many cases used lunch-times or time after their evening surgeries had ended. As well as health care workers from the NHS I wanted to interview practitioners at a local private clinic, however, they steadfastly refused my requests. The final interviewee, the feminist therapist, worked at the Women's Therapy Centre, London, and was selected because she worked outside the NHS and used what are commonly referred to as 'alternative therapies'.

The interviews were semi-structured and audio-tape recorded. In some interviews the interviewees introduced these question areas or new areas. I have not included my questions in the following chapters except for when I asked additional questions to clarify points that they were talking about during the interview. The amount of time spent on discussing each area was dependent on the interviewee, as was the introduction of any other issues. The interview duration was a minimum of fifty minutes in one instance and a maximum of two and three quarter hours in another. After each interview I made notes about the context/content of the interviews as well as documenting information that was given after the audio tape-recorder was switched off. Prior to the commencement of the interviews the interviewees approved the use of non-audio-tape-recorded material.

The work of Potter and Wetherell (1987) and Hollway (1989) on discourse methods in social psychology and the constructive role of language use informed my analysis in Chapters 4, 5 and 6. I aimed to examine the construction of anorexia nervosa in interviews with a range of health care workers because they would bring different disciplinary ideas to their

accounts. I was interested in the variability in language use in these constructions and the functions that specific language use had for the interviewees. Given the long-standing use of key ideas about anorexia nervosa,
psychopathology and women I was also interested in analysing the effects
of these constructions and the potential for the transformation of discourse
and practice.

All the interviews had been fully transcribed but to include all this
material was not necessary to the analysis. I decided to include material that
referred to the same theme but that presented the theme in different ways
because I was interested in analysing the variation within individual interviews and between interviews. For example, I used material from a psychiatric nurse's viewpoint about the types of factors that constituted a diagnosis
of anorexia nervosa rather than schizophrenia, and material from the same
nurse on this issue only when she talked about another viewpoint. I omitted
material from the same interviewee that repeated similar points about an
issue or theme because I was not interested in how many times interviewees
referred to these. Other material that I did not use was that which had constituted the development and maintenance of rapport between the interviewer and interviewee and was irrelevant to the purpose of my analysis.
Where an interviewee emphasized a word, I denote this by using italics.

The analysis was organized around grouping interview material according to key questions about anorexia nervosa, the variability between the
accounts in constructing anorexia nervosa, and the range of discourses and
themes that interviewees drew on to describe, explain or justify their practices. I analysed the interview material as it appeared within the context of
each interview, and by comparing and contrasting accounts of similar
aspects of anorexia nervosa. I was also interested in the effects of these constructions, and so following a discussion of each discourse or theme I go on
to examine their effects on women, and the reproduction of knowledge and
practice.

4
Constructions of Gender and Identity in Anorexia Nervosa

Late nineteenth century medical theories about the aetiology of anorexia nervosa heavily drew on the notion of hysteria, saturating the explanation of women, female psychology and particularly the development of women's identity. Given that the overwhelming majority of diagnoses of anorexia nervosa are of young women I was interested in the ways health care workers constructed gender and identity. I am not suggesting that the prevalence of anorexia nervosa in women does not constitute the overwhelming majority of cases, but that the construction of gender in anorexia nervosa raises key issues for the explanation of women. Two questions are of particular significance to understanding this area. First, how does the construction of anorexia nervosa as a predominantly female condition affect the clinical understanding of anorexia nervosa in males? Second, how do health care workers construct identity in theories of female psychology? In this analysis I argue that historical and social discourses about anorexia nervosa construct a series of limitations in health care workers' explanations of both males with eating disorders and non-pathological theories about women. Accordingly, I begin this analysis by providing four examples of how different health care workers construct anorexia nervosa and male patients. I then summarize the constructions in these accounts and their implications for explaining anorexia nervosa in males and females before moving on to examine anorexia nervosa and identity.

Constructions of gender and anorexia nervosa

The significance of psychiatric co-morbidity

The health care workers who worked within a hospital setting described how anorexia nervosa first came to their notice when a patient presented to the health care system with an associated illness. Anorexia nervosa may be diagnosed in patients who had been admitted to hospital for something to which it was unrelated and the associated illness continued to remain separate from the eating disorder. Here, the illness is not symptomatic of anorexia nervosa except in instances when malnutrition is present. Therefore, the first kind of associated illness, that was usually physical, brought the eating disorder to the attention of health care workers. Alternatively, if the associated illness was psychiatric it was discussed alongside the presentation of anorexia nervosa, and could be included within the discussion of the symptomatology of anorexia nervosa. Associated psychiatric illnesses included psychotic disorders; the two main disorders being schizophrenia and manic-depressive psychosis. In the first extract Dr N., a clinical psychologist, presents a case description of her only male patient with anorexia nervosa, and where psychiatric co-morbidity is also significant:

> Yes, well I think that the boy that I treated, I've only really treated one boy with anorexia nervosa, unfortunately he had an *extremely* disturbed family background. . . . A strong family history of psychiatric illness on both sides, and you know, major problems in his upbringing.
> I mean, he was *extremely* intelligent . . . so, I saw his anorexia as an attempt by him to, sort of, try and get some attention for himself. . . . It was a very destructive attempt, in the end he actually committed suicide. . . . Obviously we did consider whether he might be clinically depressed and did actually treat him with anti-depressants, but, I think, at the end of the day the problem in that instance was a major . . . sort of, intrapersonal and family problem.

Clearly this passage invokes the representation of a young man who was in a desperate struggle; so desperate that he killed himself. The diagnosis of anorexia nervosa is equated with the boy attempting to get 'some attention for himself' and the attempt is continued into describing the resultant suicide. The suicide also becomes a breaking point for the discussion of anorexia nervosa and the introduction of co-morbidity. The psychologist shifts from talking about a boy with anorexia nervosa to how she and her co-workers had considered 'whether he might be clinically depressed and did actually treat him with anti-depressants'. Suicide is not regarded as a common result of anorexia nervosa in young women whereas depression and anorexia nervosa are strongly linked. The consideration of depression by Dr N. represents an attempt to reconcile the incongruence between her diagnosis of anorexia nervosa and him 'committing suicide'. He was treated with anti-depressants, and in fact she had been treating him for depression, a condition other than that which she had diagnosed; anorexia nervosa. This move towards considering depression makes the suicide congruent with medical diagnosis. However, treatment had failed because he had died. She resolves this, in part, by returning to consider his family and this is similar to her initial description of him trying to get attention for himself. The way in which psychiatric co-morbidity is talked about in this account maintains the separateness between anorexia nervosa and depression.

The problem of self-disclosure

The long-standing status of anorexia nervosa as a predominantly female condition and relationship with a discourse of femininity may create a reluctance to diagnose the condition in males. Dr K., a clinical psychologist, constructs maleness as a barrier to the disclosure and possible diagnosis of anorexia nervosa in males:

I haven't treated any men with it [anorexia], no. I've had my suspicions occasionally, but I think it's quite difficult to get men to admit to an eating disorder. I can only think of one lad who I saw last year who had a number of again sort of social skills, self-esteem problems, who I feel his eating pattern was probably abnormal, that he was very weedy and so on, but not to the extent that I think he was anorexic, you would not necessarily label it as anorexia.

In Dr K.'s account anorexia nervosa in males is constructed as an unfamiliar occurrence, and one, in fact, that she has not treated. Although, diagnosis is not straightforward and she says 'I've had my suspicions occasionally', and locates the problem of diagnosis in relation to self-disclosure, 'I think it's quite difficult to get men to admit to an eating disorder'. In recalling a 'lad' who 'was very weedy and so on' she had not regarded the 'label' of 'anorexia' as a consequence of his presentation.

Dr K. continues:

But I think that may well be increasing. I've certainly read that it is. . . . It wouldn't surprise me. Perhaps the very body conscious, health conscious young male, who again is not quite sure perhaps of their own sexual self identity then I think it may be something to look for and probably not something that we traditionally ask and I think if you don't ask about this problem very often you don't find out because there's a whole web of secrecy around the eating rituals and patterns and thought about that and so on.

In this extract Dr K. presents identity issues as possibly contributing to anorexia nervosa in males. The problem of diagnosing male anorexia nervosa becomes, paradoxically, one obscured by social perceptions and the cultural representation of women as the group who are mostly affected by the condition which results in males' unwillingness to disclose details about their 'eating rituals'. In Dr K.'s earlier extract she identified self-disclosure as a problem in diagnosing eating disorders, yet discounts this in her diagnosis of a patient. In her second extract she emphasizes that clinicians do not traditionally ask about eating disorders, yet this is a problem already highlighted by the first extract. The extracts illustrate the structuring of the clinical interview in relation to historical and social discourses about gender and anorexia nervosa that position men as unlikely candidates for eating disorders.

Male and female anorexia nervosa

In Nurse R.'s account anorexia nervosa in males is presented in terms of its severity and this differentiates it from anorexia nervosa in females:

I think it's a lot more severe [in males] in the fact that they can . . . take it on their, out on their bodies quite a lot more *harshly* so it's a lot more a case of *starvation*. The case which I saw was a young lad who was very plump, always teased at school and all of a sudden it was just like a crash diet, and that was it, you know, he then turned anorexic, which was a shame. I haven't really seen that many cases of lads, only a couple, but they've always been much more severe and they seem much younger lads. This lad was fourteen, quite young really.

Nurse R. constructs anorexia nervosa as being different in males by describing a case of a 'young lad' through recalling her observations. She refers to three points to support her position. The severity of anorexia nervosa in males is related to the execution of anorexia nervosa that is carried out on their bodies 'more harshly'. The age of males with anorexia, in this example being fourteen years of age, makes them 'seem much younger lads', and the onset is more sudden than in females, 'and all of a sudden it was just like a crash diet, and that was it, you know, he then turned anorexic, which was a shame'. This construction of male anorexia nervosa engenders a degree of sympathy due to the severity of anorexia nervosa in 'lads', yet, Nurse R. adds the proviso, 'I haven't really seen that many cases of lads. . .', and in so doing her account avoids making generalizations.

The problem of diagnosis

Diagnosis is a fundamental process of medical practice and is fraught with difficulties within the area of mental health. These difficulties arise because psychiatric disorders are not directly observable to the practitioner except through interpretations of symptom groupings, characteristics of specific populations and behavioural classification. Further to this, a phenomenon that is classified as a psychiatric disorder, has a complex history and multiple clinical presentations, does not lend itself easily to diagnosis. Anorexia nervosa is one such phenomenon. The D.S.M. IV-R (APA, 1994) recognizes these multiple presentations and has responded by diversifying the typology of anorexia nervosa to include 'restricting type' and 'binge-eating/purging type'. Diagnosis is situated within discourses that structure ways of thinking about phenomena and practices, which, in turn, have the effect of maintaining and reproducing clinical practices. In Nurse V.'s account she describes the process of the diagnosis of anorexia nervosa in males and females and symptomatology related to her observation that diagnosis is different according to gender:

> but anorexia in men seems to be diagnosed differently anyway. It's usually put down to depression or . . . endogenous depression. I know a couple of times I've seen men with eating disorders and they haven't been diagnosed as having eating disorders. They've been diagnosed as having something like endogenous depression . . . and if you ask the consultant why is that they say, well, they've got disturbed eating patterns so that's a classic symptom, disturbed sleep and all that.

Nurse V.'s observations are characterized by the diagnosis of endogenous depression (depression arising from causes inside the body) in males rather than anorexia nervosa. The consultant's diagnosis of depression in the male patient overshadows Nurse V. having 'seen men with eating disorders and they haven't been diagnosed as having eating disorders', and she describes asking the consultant for clarification of the diagnosis. The consultant's reported response to her presented the common symptoms of depression in such a way that the symptoms confirm the diagnosis of depression rather than anorexia nervosa. Nurse V. emphasizes the similarity in the presentation of males and females, yet they become diagnosed differently.

They usually follow the same pattern as females ... people who have been diagnosed as anorexics. I mean outwardly they seem to have basically the same symptoms ... I mean disturbed sleep, disturbed eating patterns, mood swings, lack of motivation, lack of volition, lack of concentration, a very low self-esteem. The outward symptoms seem to be basically the same, but for some reason the diagnoses are different.

The smallest one that I've seen wasn't actually an anorexic patient anyway. He was supposed to be schizophrenic and he was, like, 5ft 3 inches and 4 stones, but he wasn't, again he wasn't classed as an anorexic. He was classed as schizophrenic.

Nurse V.'s description of symptoms in males and females demonstrates to her that 'outwardly they seem to have basically the same symptoms', but the 'reason the diagnoses are different' remains unclear to her. Nurse V. in making a distinction between the similarity of 'outward symptoms' leaves the possibility that internal symptoms may differentiate between gender. Nurse V.'s recollection of a male case of severe under-nutrition serves a function of further emphasizing the different diagnosis of anorexia nervosa in males and female.

Constructions of identity and anorexia nervosa

In this section I analyse the way in which health care workers constructed female identity and its relationship to anorexia nervosa. In Part I, I critically discussed the various theoretical explanations of anorexia nervosa and those in which female identity is specifically considered as a causal factor. I investigated constructions of female identity because theories of identity commonly bring the broader social and political dimensions within a concept of identity that is understood as an entity residing within individual women. Therefore, I wanted to examine the ways in which this concept of identity was constructed, its relationship with practice and effects on the representation of women diagnosed with anorexia nervosa.

Identity and control

In the following two extracts Dr M., a clinical psychologist, and Dr J., a general practitioner, present identity as being related to control and an individual's sense of autonomy. Poor control is presented as having negative effects within an anorexic's environment and the re-establishment of control is understood as a means to overcome the symptoms, develop autonomy, and produce a person who is effective within her environment.

Dr M.: I mean, I see the central issue is around control and self-identity and so on and I would say that probably broadly a psychotherapeutic approach would be likely to bring more long term results and ... really trying to help the person understand the function of their symptoms and how they're operating in, within their environment and where that may be blocking them from goals to, you know, with the focus on helping them to develop insight in that area. ...

> *Dr J.*: I think the . . . the problem is to become an autonomous adult, someone who is essentially self-governing, making your *own* decisions about your *own* life, in your *own* terms. That is a problem for everyone . . . it's a problem we'd all *half* like to opt out of because life is actually much easier if other people tell us what to do, but on the other hand it's a problem which we would . . . we also want to be like that because we want to feel we are our own boss. This is the, I mean it's an existential dilemma in fact. . . . Now, I think the . . . anorexic, what happens is . . . I don't think they start off that way but in fact their problems about becoming an autonomous adult start to hinge around the dependency problems and the power struggles over their eating. And, certainly one of the things that happens is they, a lot of them, then use those to avoid becoming an autonomous adult and I think, I mean this fits in with they won't eat because they don't want to grow breasts . . . sort of argument, do you know what I mean?

Dr J. locates the problem of identity in anorexia nervosa in the way the young woman becomes an autonomous adult. In the process of developing autonomy femininity is grappled with and/or rejected resulting in anorexia nervosa as an 'existential dilemma'. Dr J.'s representation of an 'existential dilemma' is at first presented in an apolitical, asexual way and continues to relate autonomy with a traditional psychodynamic explanation of dependency and the rejection of adult female sexuality. In Dr J.'s view for anorexics to achieve the status of becoming an 'autonomous adult' they must accept femininity, and no longer avoid eating because 'they don't want to grow breasts...'. Throughout, Dr J. constructs his account in terms of a dominant argument about anorexia nervosa that 'fits in with', 'sort of argument', and what that argument represents.

In Dr M.'s and Dr J.'s accounts control is presented quite differently. For Dr M. control was a pragmatic tool for achieving and securing goals in one's environment, whereas Dr J. talks about control as a manifestation of the anorexic woman's psychodynamics. Neither account of control brings in the social and political dimensions of what is possible or not for young women, rather the accounts located identity within individual women and the 'function of their symptoms', 'psychodynamics' and 'problems about becoming an autonomous adult'.

Identity and abuse of women

Clinical psychologist Dr M. and feminist therapist, N.J., constructed identity in relation to abuse. Dr M.:

> Another link, and I don't know how valid this is and whether I'm just obsessed with this one, but it's been my experience in dealing with people with eating disorders generally is that very often I would be looking for the idea of sexual abuse. Has there been some sort of *major* disturbance in the sense of identity and whether their body ends and another person, you know, their own boundaries. . . ?
>
>   This, this terrible sort of . . . almost not listening to sort of internal biological signals and being very confused about body shape and identity and so on. That would be in my mind too, as well.

I think it becomes a sort of false identity, doesn't it, beyond which they can shelter and that is perhaps an avoidant reaction in the same way they are avoiding certain issues that they can't cope with.

Here, based on Dr M's 'experience in dealing with people with eating disorders', she would be 'looking for the idea of sexual abuse'. Sexual abuse is put forward as being so common that this practitioner looks for it in her consultations where there is a possibility of the diagnosis of eating disorders. The focus of this clinician in looking for sexual abuse is on specific aspects of the individual person, and assumed psychological phenomena that serve as evidence of this abuse, such as 'major disturbance in the sense of identity … their own boundaries', 'not listening to sort of internal biological signals … being very confused about body shape and identity'. The act of sexual abuse and the perpetration of this abuse by another person is brought within the individual sphere and understood within this extract as an 'avoidant reaction'.

A feminist therapist provides the second example: N.J. who talks about anorexia nervosa and sexual abuse:

I think it is linked, I mean for example last year in my group of eight women, eight women had been sexually abused, but then if you look at my group this year of eight women none of them have been abused so it's just sort of in a sense I think there has been an awful lot of women who have been abused and I think there is an awful lot of women who have eating problems and I don't think that abuse causes someone to have an eating problem.

I think it is quite a big thing but I don't think it is a general rule. I think there is an awful lot of women who haven't been abused, sexually abused, but I think that that is just one form of abuse there are many other forms of abuse.

It's an interesting question, because I suppose what I see is the basic problems that a woman with an eating problem hasn't had for one reason or another enough of her mother, so that when she needs her mother, she tries to get more of her mother by using food. Now it would often be the case that in a family where sexual abuse is going on the mother will either not be around or she is certainly not doing her job in protecting her daughter from the abuse. So there will be an absent mother of some description.

This health care worker considers several forms of abuse in the development of eating problems, and sexual abuse does not constitute an aetiological factor in anorexia nervosa. The problems that a woman has with eating are directly attributable to the dynamics of the mother–daughter relationship. Sexual abuse, thus, becomes an extension of the fact that the daughter has not had her needs met by her mother. Any discussion of the woman's relationship with male family members or men was absent.

The construction of identity by means of a link with sexual abuse is made sense of in Dr M.'s account by drawing on ideas of individual psychology, whereas N.J.'s account of women and abuse focuses on women's needs that are unmet by their mothers. These accounts construct the relationship between identity and abuse in terms of psychological notions about women and 'false identity', or the psychodynamics of mothers and daughters – 'she tries to get more of her mother by using food' – that maintain a link between the individual woman, anorexia nervosa, and a pathologization of the social origins of women's abuse.

Identity and the mother–daughter relationship

For Dr J. the mother–daughter relationship is a key site of struggle about food and the developing identity of the daughter. At first he appeals to a common view of 'mums' who 'translate their love for their families into food', and that food and love 'can make you feel nice and warm inside', that establishes the connection between women and food. He describes a scenario in which there are 'mum's anxieties', there 'is a tangle of feeling', 'very strong family feelings', that is escalating and circuitous.

> To a large extent . . . I mean there's a very close connection between food and love. . . . Both can make you feel nice and warm inside . . . at a very sort of simple physical level. A lot of . . . a *large* number of mums particularly . . . translate their love for their family into food and I mean, you know . . . cooking and preparation of food is often a statement of *very* deep feeling. I mean the adverts on the telly are often saying just that – if you really love your children this is what you'll give them to eat. I think with a lot of anorexics . . . you know, I've seen certainly, there's this sort of sense that . . . that there's some sort of blackmail system . . . has been going on between mother and daughter, and typically between mother and daughter, and it *has* hinged around food . . . now it's a bit of a chicken and egg problem because whether it is that mum is anxious and pushes the food and the daughter finds this a useful way of manipulating or whether the daughter refuses food for her own personal reasons . . . enhances mum's anxieties I'm never quite sure 'cause what you meet, you know, when there's an established case so to speak, is a *tangle* of feeling. But out there, certainly there *are* very strong family feelings and they are of that sort. They are to do with whether, you know, with love and whether you, whether *she* really loves me, which ever way round that is. I think it's just a system of communication which is, which is not uncommon.

Dr J's reluctance to define the origin of the problem as being either with the mother or the daughter therefore implicates the nature of the relationship itself as being the site for the struggle. The many aspects to the escalating scenario are simplified by Dr J. finally stating 'it's just a system of communication . . . which is not uncommon'.

Dr C., a clinical psychologist:

> whatever it's worth, the dominance in the family was the mother and the need for the . . . well my guessed need . . . of the daughter to remove herself from the mother's dominating influence, it so happened were factors in both these cases, which were quite different.

Here, Dr C. tentatively describes dependency needs as a main concern in the mother–daughter relationship. Unlike Dr J. who talked about the dynamics of the relationship, Dr C. clearly identified the mothers' dominance as being the site of the problem in two cases. Dr C. introduced talk about the mother cautiously, for 'whatever it's worth', and marks her discussion of the daughter's need to separate from her 'mother's dominating influence' as the practitioner's 'guessed need' rather than a need that she assumed the daughter had.

Identity and socio-cultural pressures

The construction of identity in anorexia nervosa in relation to socio-cultural pressures presents social issues as a problem in women's achievement of a sexual identity. Dr J.:

> Women are under more pressure . . . about body shape aren't they? . . . I mean, in that sense, and if you've got a body shape problem . . . it's got to be more likely to be brought out if there's social pressures. I think that's how it is really. I don't think it's more than that.

In this extract, even though Dr J. first states that women are under more pressure about body shape, he talks about body shape problems as pre-existing problems that are separate from social pressures. The way in which body shape problems relate to social pressures is through their co-existence that makes them 'more likely to be brought out' if there are social pressures.

Dr Q., a general practitioner, presents body image as affecting eating:

> Well, I didn't even treat her. I acquired her. . . . She had got over it already so I didn't actually do anything and she came to me because of another problem. She had enormous breasts and her, because of, her body image was *so* important to her she had to have something done about this because she found that it was affecting how she felt about eating, because she was so distressed by this.
>
> I must tell you that I have in fact seen two, I had forgotten. I have in fact seen two anorexics who had to have breast reductions and this is terribly unusual. The plastic surgeon, Dr M. at the Accident, who did both operations under the National Health Service, couldn't believe it, and I had them both within a year. Both of them had been anorexic but were well coping with life now in their, sort of early twenties, but had such *huge* breast development that they just couldn't cope with what they looked like in a mirror. It was . . . affecting them and both of them had breast reductions and were much better afterwards.

Dr Q. recalls his work with two anorexics in which body image was a central concern. He describes the way he came to see these women, 'I didn't treat her', 'I acquired her', 'she'd got over it already'. He did not primarily treat them for anorexia nervosa, 'she came to me with another problem'. The women had concerns about breast size and body image that also related to eating. The problem of 'huge breast development' was something that the women were not coping with, and it was affecting their sense of who they were, because body image was 'so important to them'. Yet, a relationship between the problem and socio-cultural pressures is not made. Furthermore, the problem of two 'anorexics who had to have breast reductions' is characterized as being 'terribly unusual' and 'the plastic surgeon . . . couldn't believe it', which serves to reinforce the peculiarity of the problem and its relationship to the individual women.

Dr P., a psychiatrist, describes identity and socio-cultural pressures in terms of the effects of the media:

Obviously there is this sort of . . . pursuit of thinness, that is, sort of, . . . fashionable and idealistic . . . and that . . . teenage girls are more likely to respond to that now because . . . of the, several things, sort of, . . . sexual . . . aspects of being thin and being attractive to men . . . and I think that there is a big *media* aspect to it. . . . In men I don't think there's the same pressure, because it's a very *different*, they're in a very *different* . . . sexual position. They don't necessarily have to be . . . terribly attractive in order to go out with girls.

In this account the problems underlying anorexia nervosa are presented as external social pressures that become internal because of the way in which these pressures are responded to by young women, 'teenage girls are more likely to respond to . . .'. Dr P. constructs young women as responding to media pressures and a popular definition of attractiveness 'because they're in a very different . . . sexual position.' In this sense socio-cultural pressures have a tangible and relatively straightforward relationship to anorexia nervosa because women are trying to be thin; anorexia nervosa becomes a consequence of the 'pursuit of thinness.'

Conversely, Dr M., a clinical psychologist, describes anorexia nervosa as indicative of 'some sort of fundamental conflicts about sexuality', 'a massive complex', 'shaky self-esteem', that come into play during puberty, and draws on the notion that cultural pressures relate to women's 'obsession with their figure' that unifies all women:

I think there are often some sort of fundamental conflicts about sexuality as well, about, you know, the developmental crisis when someone is approaching puberty and so on. So, maybe a massive complex around that may be built on a very sort of shaky self-esteem really or sense of worth and feeling that their lives are very much out of control and this is one area which they can control. Plus, I think you can't afford to ignore the cultural pressures and to some extent the obsession which all women share about their figure, their appearance, their weight and so on.

The references to sexual conflicts and identity hinge around a developmental argument that assumes puberty to be problematic for women and further obfuscates the relationship between hormonal changes and young women's developing awareness of socio-cultural expectations.

The constructions of gender and anorexia nervosa in these accounts present male anorexia nervosa as different from its presentation in females, drawing on psychiatric co-morbidity, severity of weight loss, problems with self-disclosure and clinicians' questioning, as reasons for this difference. Both male patients and health care workers may be reluctant to discuss or diagnose anorexia nervosa in males due to the long-standing association between anorexia nervosa and women. The problem of self-disclosure and anorexia nervosa also involves a problem about the clinical interview and the extent to which this obscures the diagnosis of male anorexia.

If a male is diagnosed with anorexia nervosa this becomes a discursive problem because the dominant explanation of anorexia nervosa specifically links it with an ideology of femininity that has developed over the last century. One of the functions of using these strategies is that the diagnosis of an overwhelmingly female condition in males is reconciled by the fact anorexia nervosa is in some way different in males. This construction has the effect of reinforcing the notion of males as unlikely candidates for the diagnosis of anorexia nervosa. Health care workers use different strategies to try to overcome this problem in their explanations of male anorexia. The construction of masculinity in relation to anorexia nervosa, that anorexia nervosa can occur in men but is in some way different and/or more severe, emphasizes the search for different reasons for anorexia nervosa in males and females and that it is diagnosed and/or treated differently.

The constructions of identity and anorexia nervosa refer to control, abuse of women, the mother–daughter relationship and socio-cultural pressures, indicating the breadth and variability between health care workers' accounts. Anorexic women were understood as being 'out of control' of their lives and, therefore, unable to successfully develop a sexual identity, yet 'in control' of eating, to the extent that 'they behave themselves', 'but really they're still anorexic'. The link with sexual development also maintains a link with the notion that women's sexuality is always involved in some way to the onset of physical and psychological conditions. The abuse of women was explained through the notion of 'boundaries', or 'internal biological signals', and in these ways the political and social dimensions of abuse were mediated through an individual and internal dimension that functioned as a site for therapeutic intervention. One of the effects of the construction of identity as 'false identity', 'self-identity', or identity 'boundaries' is that the internal psychological dimension to which these terms refer is accessible only through certain forms of knowledge, particularly psychology and psychiatry, that is practised and maintained through the institutional position of the health professional.

Health care workers were also reluctant, and in some instances, tentative, about what they could say about anorexia nervosa. They avoided making generalizations that displayed a sensitivity to their professional identities. For these reasons the discourse of identity served a function of providing a malleable concept in health care workers' accounts. What was always unresolved in accounts that drew on social discourses of anorexia nervosa was the way in which anorexic women are both 'like all women' (Dr M.) and 'different'. The difference between women is somewhat resolved by the discourse of identity because the explanation of social pressures on women to be thin is constructed in ways that privilege individual psychology over other explanations. Consequently, the identity of an anorexic woman is constructed as always in crisis and the site where conflict is played out, making individual therapy consistent with explanation. In specific instances, when health care workers described more detail about the theories they drew on to explain anorexia nervosa these reproduced historical and dominant concepts about women, eating and psychopathology. The construction of identity to varying extents problematized women's gender identification and reproduces a pathological framework with which to work with women where identity remains a significant feature of anorexia nervosa.

The construction of gender and identity in these accounts maintains a representation of anorexia nervosa as a condition that is inextricably linked with being female and female psychology. For this reason these constructions demonstrate aspects of the discourse of femininity discussed in Chapter 2 whereby there is something essential to female psyche that predisposes women to develop anorexia nervosa. Finally, the status of not knowing the answers to questions about anorexia nervosa was emphasized by the health care workers. It is clear from these accounts that health care workers grappled with many issues of anorexia nervosa that present to them as anomalies during clinical practice.

5
The Multiplicity and Diversity of the Causes of Anorexia Nervosa

In the previous chapter I analysed constructions of gender and identity and their effects on the capacity to explain males with anorexia nervosa and non-pathological aspects of anorexia nervosa. Many of the issues that I discussed are also relevant to the numerous endeavours made by researchers, medical scientists in particular, to locate the cause of anorexia nervosa. Femininity and/or being female is a predisposing factor for diagnosis and female identity is a key construct in articulating the development of psychopathology that maintains the anorexic state. These areas of enquiry are elaborated on throughout this chapter on the multiplicity of causes of anorexia nervosa. The identification of a specific causation of anorexia nervosa has eluded scientific studies for over a hundred years, yet numerous theories of the medical, physiological, psychological, social and cultural nature of its onset exist. These theories reflect the diversification of the human sciences over the course of the twentieth century. In this chapter I analyse health care workers' constructions of anorexia nervosa in terms of explaining its causation and how they account for this diversity. In particular I focus on medical and feminist constructions of causation, and I then go on to summarize the issues that these perspectives raise for the explanation of women and treatment practices.

Medical and psychiatric perspectives on the causation of anorexia nervosa

The identification of the causes of physical and psychiatric conditions is fundamental to medical practice in order to establish appropriate treatments. The difficulties in identifying the causation of psychiatric conditions are notorious. Consequently, treatment decisions are often made post-hoc, based on conclusions drawn from observing the effects of medications or practices that are available to a practitioner. I asked each health care worker *why do people starve themselves?* Each person replied by emphasizing the difficulty of the question, but answered by recalling a plethora of 'factors', its 'multifactorial' nature, and tension between biomedical and social theories. Dr J., a general practitioner, considered whether anorexia nervosa was a psychiatric disorder in his account of causes:

> I don't know. I *really* don't know. I'm not convinced that it is in itself psychiatric. I'm *really* not. I don't think it, it's certainly not . . . psychiatric in the sense

that someone with a high level of anxiety becomes distressed because, they either, their anxiety becomes very evident or becomes attached to a particular activity. It's *not* like that. It *doesn't* seem to me psychiatric in the sense that, that a depression which responds to anti-depressants is.

In this account Dr J. constructs anorexia nervosa in terms of why it is not a psychiatric disorder by characterizing two conditions which are psychiatric and how anorexia nervosa does not fit these characterizations. The responsiveness of conditions, like depression, to medication is significant to this understanding of psychiatric classification and used to justify why anorexia nervosa is not a psychiatric condition. Dr J.:

> I'm sure some of it is genetic. I'm sure some of it is related to family dynamics. I mean . . . but to describe it as a psychiatric condition with the sort of notion that somehow if you could understand the psychodynamics that have led up to it then they'll get better I think is a nonsense.

Dr J.'s elaboration of two possible causes, genetic and family dynamics, introduces the notion of multiple and conflicting theories of anorexia nervosa, and returns to his argument against it being a psychiatric condition by charcterizing another feature of psychiatric conditions, that knowing the psychodynamics means that they will get better.

Dr J. elaborates on his observations of anorexia nervosa:

> 'cause, I mean others I've known over the years, I mean some of them stop . . . but they're still anorexics really. They control their eating. They behave themselves. They do it, but really they're still anorexic. They still think they're unbelievably fat. But there are others who have given it up and I think the girl I spoke to, the one I said, who came back with her two children, I don't think she is anorexic any more, truly not anorexic . . . she's very slightly plump, I mean very nicely plump, just right you could argue, but she is slightly plump and she thinks she's the right thickness.

Dr J. differentiates between anorexics in terms of those who are 'still anorexics really' and an example of a 'girl' who was 'truly not anorexic' and 'came back [to him] with her two children'. Dr J., in stating 'they control their eating', 'they behave themselves', 'they do it, but really they're still anorexic. They still think they're unbelieveably fat' introduces an issue of deceit in the anorexic women's 'behaviour' and thinking' that the medical practitioner has identified. The key feature of the recovered state is being 'very nicely plump' and the apparent agreement between Dr J. and the woman that she is the 'right thickness' enables the relinquishment of the diagnosis of anorexia nervosa.

Dr Q., a general practitioner, states:

> I don't know. I don't know if anyone knows. I mean maybe it's this . . . distorted body image, thing, striving for perfection in what you look like.

Dr P., a psychiatrist:

> I would view it as being really multiple causes. I have some difficulty in seeing it purely as an organic brain disorder with disturbance of hormones. I think that may be a *result* of rather than a cause of anorexia nervosa. There's no doubt that there is hormonal disturbance and that it is in the hypothalamic pituitary axis,

but it is *very* difficult to actually say with any degree of certainty that is the actual cause of it.

In this account Dr P. uses a justificatory position for the lack of an identifiable causation that states what anorexia nervosa is not rather than attributing it to a hormonal cause. Dr P.'s notion that there are multiple causes results in her viewing anorexia nervosa as a 'multifactorial condition'. The comparison of anorexic symptomatology with paranoid delusion functions to maintain a psychiatric framework through which anorexia nervosa is understood by this psychiatrist. By employing the criteria for paranoid delusion, anorexia nervosa is made explicable to this health care practitioner, and the uncertainty about the multifactorial nature and the complexity that that presents for interventions is, in part, overcome. Dr P. again:

> There are the sort of intrapersonal and interpersonal causes which I think have to be taken into consideration so I really view it as a multifactorial condition, rather than a single, biological entity. To me there is very little difference between this distortion of body concept which all anorexics have and someone with a paranoid delusion who holds on to it, believes in it firmly, *cannot* be rationalized out of it, and is unprepared to believe there is any other explanation for it. I mean, this distortion of body image fits the criteria for delusion, so I certainly feel that is delusion.

The identification of perceptual distortion is a common factor associated with anorexia nervosa. Other interpretations of perceptual distortion as a distortion of body concept related to socio-cultural expectations of young women to be slim/thin and that encourage constant dissatisfaction with body size is absent. Dr P., like Dr J. earlier, attempts to explain anorexia nervosa by referring to another psychiatric category. Dr P. compares the similarity between one symptom of anorexia nervosa, distortion of body concept, with paranoid delusion, associated with either schizophrenia or manic-depressive psychosis. In making this comparison Dr P. identifies the medication chlorpromazine, a treatment for psychoses, as a treatment for anorexia nervosa:

> Chlorpromazine, for example, is in fact an anti-psychotic as well as a major tranquilliser, but it's not really used for that because I don't think that most psychiatrists, don't view this distorted body image as delusional.

> [*Interviewer*: If psychiatrists treated it as delusional would they use chlorpromazine?]

> Well, you could use more potent anti-psychotics, but of course they would have side-effects and then you also have to deal with the other problems of weight. But I have often wondered what would happen if I actually gave someone a very potent anti-psychotic . . . particularly if they were inpatients.

Despite being unsure about the causes and symptoms of anorexia nervosa Dr P. has an interest in investigating the relationship between a potent antipsychotic drug and anorexia nervosa. Psychiatric discourse maintains this practice of investigation by developing an understanding of conditions by observing their responsiveness to medication.

In the following extracts health care workers put forward the multifactorial model in responses to the definition of causation. These responses result in an oscillation between the singularity and multiplicity of causation. Dr H., a psychiatrist, describes a multifactorial theory of anorexia nervosa:

> very difficult question [causation]. I wish I could *answer that* ... straight-forward, simple answer is I don't know the correct answer, but I think it's a multifactorial causation. There are certainly psychological factors, social factors and maybe an organic factor.
>
> ... discarding all this it may have an organic basis, mainly because some of the symptoms, like mainly the cessation of menstruation and ... some of these features could be an endocrine or hormonal imbalance in some way causing the problems. So, in fact, I'm really not sure what the actual causation ... but it seems to be very many factors and it's a very *complex* problem that we are dealing with, and quite often in treating the anorexic the main problem is that we do not *know* which area to stress or where to treat.

Here, Dr H. avoids specifying a cause, he says 'I don't know', 'I think it's ... multifactorial', and lists several possible causes, he uses 'may', 'could be' to describe and play down biological bases of anorexia. These ways of talking produce an account in which not knowing is restated. The strategy of not knowing is evident, and his reference to 'actual causation' is used as a contrast and upshot of his deliberations, together with 'it's complex', as a warrant for not knowing. In these ways the accounts do not reinforce a single causative theory of anorexia nervosa.

Clinical psychologist Dr M. talks about multifactorial causes:

> Oh, dear me! I wish I knew. I wish I knew about that actually ... I think it's many and various. I mean there is this sort of hypothesis isn't there and there's some sort of biological link ... not wonderfully convinced of that idea. I mean I think there are central issues around personal control, how someone sees control. The whole issue of controlling their lives which I think it seems to be more of a problem for women. Though I think it would be unlikely if that problem did not develop within the context of some quite stirred family relationships. . . . I think there are often some sort of fundamental conflicts about sexuality as well, about, you know, the developmental crisis when someone is approaching puberty and so on. So, maybe a massive complex around that may be built on a very sort of shaky self-esteem really or sense of worth and feeling that their lives are very much out of control and this is one area which they can control. Plus, I think you can't afford to ignore the cultural pressures and to some extent the obsession which all women share about their figure, their appearance, their weight and so on. This is where I have in mind, you know, you have to look at things like a spectrum condition. It may well be that what maintains it I don't know, I mean you probably know more about this than I do, but this idea of a *high*, you know, that if you do lose weight or go without food for a while that maybe there's a certain biochemical kind of aspect which comes into it and it's also a very *powerful* way to, sort of, control relationships indirectly for somebody who is ... whose assertion skills are not particularly well developed in other areas.

Dr M.'s account of the causes of anorexia nervosa involves a similar pattern to that of Dr H. For Dr M. some of the factors that contribute to anorexia nervosa include 'personal control', 'family discord', 'sexuality' and 'cultural pressures', and the biological link is understood as a factor that maintains rather than causes anorexia nervosa. The notion of factors that maintain behaviours contrasts with the common cause–effect relationship within medical science. The interrelations between physiological and psychological processes become clearly positioned in these extracts and related to either causative or maintenance roles in anorexia nervosa. The diverse explanations of the causes and symptoms of anorexia nervosa contribute to its status as a complex condition. This complexity becomes compounded through multiple explanations of causes, factors and symptoms, as being either primary or secondary to the onset of anorexia and understood within the specific disciplinary frameworks of different health care workers.

In clinical psychologist Dr C.'s account 'different factors', 'cultural conditions', 'psychological influences' and 'family dynamics' may be important in anorexia nervosa.

> I'm not sure. I think there are a lot of factors involved and different factors play a different ... importance for people who experience anorexia. I think there's a general cultural background, particular socio-cultural pressures on women in terms of valuing themselves in terms of their body. On top of these cultural conditions I think there's various ... kind of psychological influences, for example, family dynamics may be important ... some people argue for a genetic component. I am sceptical about that.

As well as drawing on a multifactorial model of anorexia nervosa Dr C. also uses a socio-cultural explanation with reference to body image, rather than perceptual distortion. Dr C. introduces the notion that different factors have different importance for people. The notion of relative factors contrasted with the traditional view that the aetiology of anorexia nervosa is 'discoverable' shows how the search for a causation for anorexia nervosa may also mask a consideration of the relative significance of factors in relation to individual cases.

I asked two psychiatric nurses who worked as primary nurses to patients diagnosed with anorexia nervosa, *Why do people starve themselves?* In Nurse T.'s account media influences on people in terms of what 'you have to be' becomes translated into individual behaviour. Media pressures advocate that eating little is being 'good', 'trim' and 'fit', and this is translated into 'they all seem to be vegetarians', 'they quite often go into a gym', but they become unlike other people who do this because people with an eating disorder 'go over the top'.

> From the various people I've seen which I consider to just have an eating disorder I would say there's quite a lot of, at the moment, sort of media influence. You have to, have to be good and trim, fit and, you know, eat healthily and they all seem to be either vegetarians, vegans, into wholefood diets. . . . They quite often go into a gym, into keeping fit, jogging, whatever. So they seem very, sort of, influenced by today's trends if you like, but go over the top.

In Nurse X.'s account anorexia nervosa is 'a way of getting attention within a family that's having problems'.

> There's no hard and fast aetiology. There's a lot of causes from what I've seen anyway. Usually they're overweight or have been overweight at some point in their lives, or some people say it's due to attention seeking. It's a way of getting attention within a family that's having problems. The father's away a lot or the mother's away a lot. I know at the clinic where I work ... about 80 per cent of

the girls that I've seen with anorexia, it's strange that their fathers work abroad a lot or have got jobs where they're away from home a lot.

The patient is brought within the clinical domain through the notion that anorexia nervosa has multiple causes, complexities and uncertainties that manifest within individual psychology. In this way there is consensus between health care workers' accounts of what constitutes anorexia nervosa. A major distinction between the nurses' articulation of anorexia nervosa and earlier accounts made by medical practitioners and psychiatrists is that the nurses drew on their direct observations of patients. Unlike medical accounts the nurses did not refer directly to psychopathological explanations.

A feminist perspective on the causation of anorexia nervosa

The following extracts are from an interview with a feminist therapist from the Women's Therapy Centre (WTC) in London, UK. The work of Susie Orbach and co-therapists forms a key theoretical foundation to the work at the Centre. During the initial part of the interview the therapist, N.J., defined her therapy for me as being a combination of art therapy and feminist therapy that has a psychoanalytic orientation. Because N.J. has particular expertise in the provision of therapy for eating disorders I asked her the question: *Why do people starve themselves?*

> That's a jolly big question. Well, in a nutshell I would answer you by saying I think it's to do with the mother–daughter relationship and that's a fairly classic feminist psycho-therapy viewpoint, I fairly closely follow Susie [Orbach] or I sort of agree with her analysis of the problem. Within a context of a patriarchal society, I mean I think trying to kind of pull teeth out with threads with all of that is quite tricky. I suppose what I think is that because we live in a patriarchal society where men at least hold the external power in relationships between men and women, women then get locked into a position of both taking care of others and therefore their own needs get put aside, and so I think their needs kind of get split off, and thought of as bad.

N.J.'s account of self-starvation is explicitly situated with reference to theory. She makes this theoretical framework clear in her explication of the mother–daughter relationship, patriarchal social structure, and women's denial of their needs, focusing on the denial of nutrition needs. In this account she privileges the mother–daughter relationship as the nexus for the psychoanalytic interpretation of anorexia nervosa. N.J. continues:

> I mean, I think it also is very much wound up with Christian ethic and I think that the myth of creation has a lot to answer for. I think it's very deeply embedded in the way in which we view black and white for example, and sexuality and pleasures of the flesh and I think women end up being the scapegoats for, well if you like, being the ones in a sense who are seen to be the temptresses. Men can go off and enjoy themselves and it's absolutely fine, a stud, but for a woman to do that she is seen as a whore and somehow this whole business is, we've got to keep the lid on women's power. We've got to reduce their appetites. We've got to reduce both their eating appetites and their sensual and

sexual appetites. I think in the last century, their sexuality was very much sort of bound up, tied up, cut off, surgically removed.

In this extract morality and women's sexuality presents a social dilemma. Women's power, situated within female sexual consciousness, is defined by males in patriarchal societies in such a way whereby women's sexuality ends up being regarded negatively and something that should be contained. The result, N.J. states, is that 'women end up as scapegoats' for the behaviour of men. The process of scapegoating is a strategy that enables the ills of a society to be made attributable to an object or social group. From a feminist psychoanalytic perspective, therapist N.J. explicates the effects of patriarchal society as imposing the need to reduce women's appetite for both eating and sexuality, that is successfully achieved through the subjugation of women.

Feminist therapist N.J. continues:

So in a very subtle way, I think women's power is thought of by the whole society I think as very frightening in the image of this huge devouring mother, where and which everyone comes from and somehow everyone is scared of that and wants to push that image away, so that it would get reduced in size, they want to reduce their power, feel bad about their power, feel bad about their needs, feel bad about depending. And how that then ties into the mother–daughter relationship and working with that on a very personal basis in therapy.

I understand it as being passed down, generation to generation, and that I, as a therapist and as a feminist therapist, it is my job to somehow try and enable that woman through my relationship with her to understand how she is re-enacting this with her mother to somehow try and get her out of that a bit, but also to put it in a context in a very subtle way of the society to help her to understand that she is not this isolated being.

In N.J.'s extracts the symbolic dimension of anorexia nervosa is a drama related to women's social position and played out within the mother–daughter relationship. Because of the focus on the mother–daughter relationship I asked N.J. the following question: *What do you think about the criticism of this approach because it seems to blame the mother for the daughter's conflict?* She replied:

I don't really blame them. You see I think this is very interesting the word 'blame', and a lot of my clients can't talk about how their mothers treated them because they are so scared of blaming them, and it's like remove the word blame, well this is what happened and no one is ready to blame but let's look at your feelings about what happened.

I see anorexia as being literally a self-imposed starvation. I mean there is all sorts of physical symptoms that come with that which I don't necessarily ask a woman about or look for, I mean, like the menstruation stopping. I mean I suppose I just look for when a woman is obviously starving herself. I see this as being like a continuum. I see anorexia as being the most extreme in the sense that I think the woman is very much cut off and trying to make some kind of, trying to build herself a completely self-contained world, so that she doesn't need anything from anyone else, but of course, her dependency needs are enormous and so she creates a situation so that eventually she probably gets hospitalized or she then gets herself into a situation where she actually has to be looked after by other people round the clock. Then I would see the movement bulimia as being the point at which actually she can't deny any longer and so bingeing breaks out. I would see a movement into bingeing and vomiting as progress and also that would also symbolize capacity for her to actually take things in, relationship wise, so that if she started to come to see me as a therapist then her movement and bingeing would also symbolize her capacity to relate to me and that something has penetrated her from the outside world so to speak.

N.J. describes how a woman's symbolic use of food involves a continuum of eating disorders. Anorexia nervosa is at one end of the spectrum and symbolic of unmet needs and the self-imposed isolation from the woman's need to ask for anything and draw attention to her needs when in fact she has enormous needs. Bulimia nervosa is construed as movement, and 'vomiting as progress . . . that would also symbolize capacity for her to actually take things in, relationship wise'. In contrast to the construction of anorexia nervosa through symbolic interpretations and a continuum of eating disorders, psychiatric discourse constructs these disorders as separate conditions and categories. A patient who is diagnosed as suffering from one category may have symptoms of another, but they are not generally considered together. Interestingly, N.J. constructs bulimia nervosa as being a 'progression' in the woman's development.

Health care workers' accounts constructed anorexia nervosa in ways that avoided specifying a causation. The various strategies that health care workers' used were 'not knowing' the cause of anorexia nervosa, with an emphasis on 'I don't know if anyone knows' as an appeal to the overwhelming nature of the problem. Anorexia nervosa was constructed in terms of a multifactorial causation or model, or a list of the possible causes, including hormonal dysfunction, genetic, socio-cultural pressures and family dynamics. Terms such as 'may' or 'could be' were used to describe and play down the biological bases of anorexia nervosa. The status of anorexia nervosa as being 'complex' was a key justification for 'not knowing.'

Also anorexia nervosa was constructed in terms of its status as a psychiatric condition, that involved various characterizations of psychiatric categories in order to compare the symptoms rather than the causes. For example, perceptual distortion, a symptom of anorexia nervosa, was compared with paranoid delusion and psychotic conditions. The construction of causation and symptomatology of anorexia nervosa through multiple discourses creates and maintains the status of anorexia nervosa as a 'complex' condition. This complexity has the effect of justifying the investigation of new ideas about causation. These investigative or other practices will be consistent with the discourse within which the ideas emanate, and in the instance of psychiatry, take the form of investigating the responsiveness of anorexia nervosa to anti-psychotic medication. In contrast, feminist therapist, N.J., constructed anorexia nervosa in terms of a symbolic interpretation of women's unmet needs. Feminist discourse was structured in this account in ways that involved broader social and political dimensions of anorexia nervosa, yet, like medical and psychiatric discourses, brought women within the clinical and therapeutic arena for treatment of individual psychology.

All the health care workers drew on the separation between individuals and social practices. In medical and psychiatric accounts of the causation of anorexia nervosa there is an assumed and individualized psychopathology/psychology of the patient where socio-cultural factors, such as the family arena or social pressures, are external influences. The separation between individual and society and anorexia nervosa is particularly problematic. While there is a shifting consensus from various disciplines towards the social explanation of anorexia nervosa there is a lack of social theorization within medical psychiatric and feminist discourses about changing therapeutic practices. Social factors are regarded as influences on the individual that cause distress and psychological dysfunction. Further to this, the management and explanation of anorexia nervosa are continually bound together within medical discourse because the physical complications arising from malnutrition require necessary medical assistance. The confusion surrounding the primary or secondary onset of physical symptoms within medical discourse continues to complicate the socio-cultural explanation of anorexia nervosa. A major consequence of this is that while anorexia nervosa continues to be managed by the medical and psychiatric professions social explanations and practices remain on the periphery.

6
Clinical Treatments for Anorexia Nervosa

I critically examined the emergence of the clinic and modern hospital in Chapter 1 and the way in which the hospital facilitated the medical and psychiatric management of anorexia nervosa. This form of institutional management of anorexic women remains today although the restructuring of psychiatric services during the 1980s has created a shift in policy away from hospital care towards 'community care'. Women and men who refuse food to varying extents and have significant weight loss, after no organic causation is found, may be diagnosed with anorexia nervosa. Most commonly this diagnosis is based on the classification of anorexia nervosa provided in the American Psychiatric Association's *Diagnostic and Statistical Manual of Mental Disorders IV* (1994). Those with less severe weight loss are also managed through the hospital as outpatients, yet, like inpatients, their weight loss is clinically monitored and severe loss remains the major criterion for admission to hospital.

The range of health care workers who are involved in the clinical management of a person diagnosed with anorexia nervosa, commonly include two or more of the following: general practitioner, consultant/psychiatrist, psychiatric nurse, psychologist, social worker, dietitian and counsellor. Medical practitioners authorize the type of clinical management, determine referral processes, treatment interventions, and hospital admission and discharge. However, the diagnosis and clinical management of anorexia nervosa is not a simple reflection of medical procedures rather, these procedures are constructed in specific ways and position the person who is diagnosed as a subject of institutional practices. I was interested in the construction of clinical practices and ways in which institutional structures, such as the hospital, continued to facilitate the management of anorexia nervosa and the effects on patients. During the interviews health care workers provided descriptions of their clinical practice that related to three main areas; (1) hospital admission and procedures, (2) therapies, and (3) recovery, and their accounts demonstrate the ways in which the clinic is maintained as a key site for treatment.

Hospital admission and procedures

Severe weight loss precipitates the admission of a person to hospital and the diagnosis of anorexia nervosa. The general practitioner, hospital physician and/or a psychiatrist make the diagnostic decision. Hospitalization can be voluntary or, for example, in the UK involuntary hospitalization is secured under the 1983 Mental Health Act. In the following accounts two psychiatric nurses construct clinical treatments for anorexia nervosa characterized by two main objectives: observation and assessment of patients and establishment of weight gain. Nurse X. describes the admission of anorexic patients.

> Well, when they come in they're usually assessed for the first few days to take a baseline really, . . . all their behaviour, their eating behaviour especially, to see how much they eat, *when* they eat, and things like moods and sleep. Then, after that . . . we usually draw up a menu. . . . I mean food is a central part of their treatment and they draw up menus of things that they like and dislike. Then, they're usually isolated in a room . . . the bathroom doors are locked, someone sits with them 24 hours a day . . . special nursing it's called . . . and they start off with small portions and the portions get bigger. It starts off with three light dinners, then the portions and the meals themselves get more substantial as they improve.
>
> Basically it revolves around getting them to eat and getting them to keep the food down because apparently they . . . the consultants' main worry is the *deviousness* of them. . . . Because they claim that they're devious and somebody needs to sit with them after they've eaten at least for one hour afterwards . . . because they will regurgitate this food or they take laxatives or they'll exercise, you know, burn off this, all this food. The main emphasis in the treatment really is to get them to keep food down, to get them to put on weight and weight gain is a measure of success of treatment really.

Anorexia nervosa is constructed as a problem of weight loss and the hospital treatment programme is structured in ways that facilitate patients' weight gains. On admission to hospital, as Nurse X. described, 'they're usually assessed . . . all their behaviour, their eating behaviour especially', 'we draw up a menu', 'I mean food is a central part of their treatment'. While the main focus of treatment is on the patient's increased food consumption, 'getting them to keep food down' is presented as a major problem. The notion of 'special nursing' is introduced and has a range of functions that revolve around surveillance including, and for obvious reasons, monitoring severely low weight patients. However, the practice of surveillance is based on the health care workers' distrust of anorexic patients because they are 'devious', 'they will regurgitate this food or they take laxatives or they'll exercise'. The nurse also becomes a subject of this representation of anorexics by having to carry out practices to prevent them from not keeping food down, or as punishment for their deceit. The practices described as follows, 'they're usually isolated in a room . . . the bathroom doors are locked, someone sits with them 24 hours a day', are justified in these accounts because patient characteristics are presented as being inherent to a psychopathology of anorexia nervosa.

The emphasis on food and weight gain is characterized by a psychological struggle between these nurses and patients. Psychiatric Nurse T. describes her work with an anorexic woman:

> with the anorexic patient, or a patient with an eating disorder, we tend to find that even though we do work on the primary nurse system we have to keep the other staff totally informed of *every* development, because we found that manipulation is a particularly difficult aspect. There was a lot of manipulation, hence we found one girl to have kidney beans at the bottom of her locker, raw kidney beans which she fed herself on, 'cause it's a good, you know, laxative. Also, sending other patients down the shops for laxatives, having loads and loads and loads of fruit and bread, bingeing at night in order that she could be weighed the next day so that she would gain the weight she'd have a bottle of Perrier water plus a loaf of bread the night before a weigh. Hence we had to make sure that we had different weight days. We could never tell her when she was going to be weighed. So you always come across these conditions which you're never really prepared for as a nurse, you just can't think ahead of them so you've always got to think, come across them and then have to eradicate the problem like we do. . . . You would have to sit her down, ask her why, if she'd got any more . . . search her room with her and another nurse, . . . with her permission, if, you know, it's . . . it's very difficult, especially as that time, sort of, building up a relationship with her and then you've got to do that.

Clinical treatment is defined by the antagonism between the nurse and patient in which there is a struggle over weight gain, eating, and 'keeping food down'; the antithesis of anorexia nervosa. Nurse T. describes how this treatment regime is practised and is again justified in terms of the patient's characteristics, 'because we found that manipulation was a particularly difficult aspect'. The vivid description of 'one girl' who had 'kidney beans at the bottom of her locker' reinforces the difficulty of patients that the nurse works with as well as the implications that this has for the nurse in building a relationship with the patient. The focus on food and weight gain constructs an elaboration of eating rituals, food avoidance, weight gains and surveillance that is structured through hospital procedures and clinical goals.

Therapies

Two forms of therapy are used with anorexic patients; naso-gastric feeding/drugs and/or psychotherapy. The clinical focus on patients establishing weight gain is highlighted in the following accounts where the practices of patient bed rest, to minimize the expenditure of calories, and behavioural therapy are presented by psychiatric Nurse T:

> Well, I'll take the one recent case. What we did for her, which was probably best really. She was *extremely* underweight. . . . She really wasn't eating adequately so we made sure a nursing point of view, monitoring her weight initially. We liaised with the doctor. The doctor was quite firm, took the *firm* approach really, because she was literally on death's door. If she'd lost any more weight then she'd end up in _____ Hospital being tube-fed. We've never tube-fed here, as such, what we were doing was saying look, you know you've got to rest. So she had a single room. We confined her to that room. She rested

on her bed for the majority of the time. She only came out for eating. . . . She, she was occupied, but didn't really restrict her movements too much, we just didn't like her moving around too much 'til she gained the weight. We liaised with the dietician to make sure that she got high protein foods. She was pre-scribed Fortical. . . . She was prescribed all sorts of vitamin tablets. She had Build-Up at regular intervals. She had snacks and the kitchens were very good. We had to liaise with the kitchens in order that they could bring special food.

In this account the nurses' practices are presented as a result of a physician's decision about treatment, 'the doctor was quite firm, took the *firm* approach really, because she was literally on death's door'. The patient is isolated, her movements restricted and she is fed milk-based meal replacement drinks such as 'Fortical' and 'Build-up'. The 'firm approach' is one characterized by practices focused exclusively on weight gain and control of the patient, 'so she had a single room', 'we confined her to that room', 'we just didn't like her moving around too much 'til she gained the weight', and in which the patient is positioned as a passive recipient of this clinical regime. Nurse T. continues:

From there, once she had gained the weight and we knew she had a target weight. She knew the weight she had to gain, she could come out more and she liked that better. She could move around the ward. So we were acting on like a reward basis really. Once she could move around the ward, then we had another target weight when she could go down to the telephone and. . . . If she didn't reach this couple of pounds target weight then that privilege would be taken away. And she did strive to gaining, say, a healthy, reasonable weight. She didn't improve drastically, but it was healthier.

Nurse X. elaborates on the reward system:

If they put on weight they can have certain privileges, like, if they put on, say 4–5lbs by the end of the week then they're allowed to go home for the weekend or they're allowed to do something that they like doing.

The behavioural approach to the treatment of anorexia nervosa is based on the most simplified form of conceptualizing human actions. A person is housed in an environment of deprivation only to make additions to this state through compliance with designated rules. A system of privileges and rewards is offered to the patient for exhibiting specific behavioural goals, in this instance those being food consumption leading to weight gain, but these rewards are then withdrawn if an observation of non-compliant patient behaviour is made. The relationship between the nurse and the anorexic woman is structured vis-à-vis weight gain, 'she knew the weight she had to gain, she could come out more and she liked that better. She could move around the ward. So we were acting on like a reward basis really', in which the patient becomes isolated, observed, measured and governed, according to a schedule of clinically determined goals. 'Once she could move around the ward, then we had another target weight when she could go down to the telephone and. . . . If she didn't reach this couple of pounds target weight then that privilege would be taken away.'

The hospital structures the treatment of patients around food and weight related behaviours as individual entities and in doing this drastically limits the type of information and knowledge that both clinicians and patients draw on to make decisions about food, weight, and body size. These practices allow for the monitoring and intense surveillance of the patient, yet simultaneously displace the complexities and breadth of the patient's life.

One of the greatest obstacles to the adoption of a behavioural approach is the patient's agreement. The 'contract' is a common means of introducing the patient to treatment as psychiatrist, Dr P., describes in his account:

> I mean, if they were *seriously*, very much underweight and any physical activity was going to be detrimental then obviously we would have to have a contract whereby they actually *did remain* in *bed*, and that their meals were supervised. I mean, certainly I do believe in the contract basis because I think that it's *very, very* difficult to engage any anorexic in ... treatment. They are usually *extremely* resistant to any kind of treatment and so I think that the contract is one way of trying to ... let them know that they *can* have choice in what ... or not.
>
> ... it would be based on behavioural methods whereby they would be rewarded and obviously we have to find out what sort of things they like, in terms of activities, or in terms of ... foods, or, you know, something specific that they really enjoy doing or having ... and that, you know, can be built into the whole contract contingent on weight gain. They do need to understand that ... not so contingent on eating meals, but contingent on gaining a certain amount of weight which is agreed with them ... beforehand.
>
> One thing ... maybe I should mention. ... The one thing that I have come across in common with most of the anorexics is ... resistance to whatever you have to offer. I think if you can overcome that resistance ... working with them it is much easier, but resistance is something I've found in common to all of them and rather difficult to overcome ... and if you had a way of overcoming that, if there was a simple way of getting over that initial, ... then treatment would become much easier.

Nurse T.:

> She always knew what she was striving for, what goal we had and it was always a goal which was discussed with her. We said four pounds and she felt it was unrealistic then we would try and come to a happy medium, 'cause it's no good if she didn't agree.

Clinical treatment is presented as being underpinned by the notion that a patient has a choice about its course and is agreed upon through the use of the contract. 'They are usually *extremely* resistant to any kind of treatment and so I think that the contract is one way of trying to ... let them know that they *can* have choice in what ... or not.' The difficulty of working with anorexics is emphasized in these accounts through their representation of being 'resistant'. Of course, the 'contract' only works with 'compliant' patients and dilemmas arise when a patient will not enter into any negotiation about weight gain. This approach compresses a number of moral, social and ethical aspects of clinical interventions into a form whereby patients are evaluated in terms of the framework of normative behaviourism. The use of the contract thereby reduces the complexities of anorexia nervosa and its treatment to a model of human behaviour where the complications become replaced within the clinic by a set of requisite conditions that need to be met for a successful outcome. Resistance to treatment as demonstrated in these extracts presents a profound dilemma for the medical profession when the patient is at a very low body weight and at risk of dying.

Psychiatrist, Dr H., describes the time when a physician has to decide about whether to intervene with a re-feeding programme, and introduces the problematic issue of 'naso-gastric' or 'force-feeding':

> Very severe cases with gross weight loss which could be almost life-threatening at that stage I'd prefer to treat them on a medical ward with the help of a physician . . . there the emphasis would be on the patient regaining some of the weight that has been lost . . . and at that stage maybe more psychological forms of treatment can be undertaken, but, *initially* the *primary* concern would be to *get* some weight back on so that it doesn't lead to more physical problems.
>   . . . it may even be intravenous nutrition at some stage where . . . they are not given oral food or nutrition and . . . also orally a strict regime, sometimes even by gastric feeding to get their weight back to normal, back to *some* sort of acceptable level.
>   . . . it may even be tube-feeding with some very severe cases, but generally that may not be necessary. They will be able to eat under supervision and regain their weight, but I'm talking about extreme cases where they may need tube-feeding, yes.

Dr H. talked about acute cases of anorexia nervosa when the use of tube feeding is considered. The objective of tube feeding was for him to: '*get* some weight back on' to avoid 'more physical problems'; get weight back to '*some* sort of acceptable level'; and to be used with 'extreme cases'. The patient's weight, in these extracts, is clearly pivotal for Dr H. choosing a treatment option. The separation of very low weight anorexics from others also involved a demarcation between the psychiatrist and when he worked with a physician.

Psychiatrist Dr P. talks reservedly about tube-feeding:

> If it were *that bad* then they would clearly need to be in . . . a medical unit . . . but actually I would have grave doubts about pushing the whole tube-feeding business. I think that it isn't very easy, it isn't easy, to sort of watch someone starving themselves . . . but, equally, *how* much of . . . force-feeding, as it were, is actually going to help *them* to see things differently. I don't know there's a major, sort of, ethical and moral aspect to this and I don't have any . . . answers to it. There's obviously many different views on it.

In contrast to Dr H., Dr P. introduced the ethical and moral aspects of force-feeding and expressed reservations about its use because he does not know to what extent this practice affects the patient's thinking about eating, whether it will help, 'them to see things differently', and its use in this account is not only related to the clinical imperative of patient weight gain. The administration of force-feeding is also presented as an ultimatum given to patients who are at risk of losing more weight as Nurse T. describes:

> She came here on the understanding that if she lost any more weight then she would go to _____ Hospital and be tube-fed or she could accept help and come as an informal patient here and more or less have counselling. . . .

Here, force-feeding is used as an instrument of punishment, as the most severe intervention, if the patient lost any more weight. The patient's acceptance of the clinical alternative, 'counselling', is presented as a way of preventing this from happening to her, and 'she could accept help and come as an informal patient'.

One psychiatric nurse explained to me outside the interview that thirty five kilos and below was proposed as the working definition of when an individual's life was considered as being under threat from starvation. At this weight a medical practitioner is able to enforce compulsory treatment in the UK by 'sectioning' an individual under the Mental Health Act, 1983. With the authorization of a medical officer the patient can be legally held within a psychiatric/general hospital for 72 hours and given treatment ranging from drugs to one prescribed treatment of electro-convulsive therapy.

Recovery

Within the clinic weight gain is the most significant treatment outcome. The measurement of recovery is relative to the establishment of weight within an approximate range for age and height, as well as the duration of its maintenance. The notion of recovery from anorexia nervosa is complex. In the clinic recovery from anorexia nervosa involves a major distinction between short term and long term outcomes. Psychiatrist Dr H.states:

> I think . . . in long-term recovery or the long term it has generally been not very good. . . . In the immediate, if you look at maybe their putting the weight back on or doing well for the short term, yes, it's been reasonable, with various strict regimes. But, in the long term, I think it's generally been disappointing.

Clinical Psychologist Dr M.:

> I certainly have been involved in the sort of analysis of . . . some people who have presented with problems of anorexia but my success rate on it I think is . . . fairly low. I found that either people tend to drop out of treatment or haven't been particularly responsive to the kind of approach that I've adopted . . . which has made me a little bit pessimistic in parts I guess. . . .

In these extracts two possibilities about recovery from anorexia nervosa are proposed, one that confirms the poor long term outcome of recovery, the other is linked to people tending to 'drop out' or 'haven't been particularly responsive to the kind of approach' adopted by the clinician. The lack of treatment success is not presented clearly as a problem of the limits of treatment. In the extract below Dr H. is responding to my question about whether any patients had died.

> No, not any of mine. No. No. That is generally because of other complications because quite a few of them seem to have other difficulties. There are other problems . . . deliberate self-harm apart from anorexia, depressive illness co-inciding with anorexia. So, I think even when that happens it's, it's maybe because of other complications, other co-existing problems.

Dr J.'s, a general practitioner, response to this question was:

> I mean, anorexia is life-threatening. I've known a patient die of anorexia when I was at the _____ Hospital. They had someone die. . . . If you, if you don't take, . . . you know, you'll lose them.

Dr H.'s talk about fatality and anorexia nervosa uses a strategy that separates the possibility of death from anorexia nervosa by attributing examples of fatality to other complications, 'other problems . . . apart from anorexia', 'other co-existing problems' and not as a result of anorexia. Anorexia nervosa, in this example, is constructed like earlier examples in such a way that maintains a separation between it and other problems or psychiatric categories. In contrast to this Dr J. talks about death from anorexia nervosa being a very real possibility. However, both medical practitioners, having many years' experience, gave no account during the interviews of any complications arising from the management of anorexic patients, particularly in relation to the practice of gastric feeding or when there is no patient consent to treatment. Further to this, Dr J. decided to provide more detail to me when the audio tape-recorder was turned off, and I was taking only field notes. Dr J., described the complications that had arisen from tube-feeding one of his patients that he had mentioned earlier. She had weighed approximately twenty nine kilos on the commencement of tube-feeding. She had not eaten regular meals for a very long period of time, and was used to surviving on small intakes of food and drinks. On her admission to hospital she was prescribed naso-gastric feeding with a high calorie milk based food substitute which caused gastric and intestinal complications and was shortly followed by her death. The expression of this detail is significant due to the practitioner's choice of timing when to speak about his patient, and his accompanying sadness as he recalled this young woman.

By examining these accounts I have shown the ways in which health care workers construct their clinical practices and the various strategies that are used to justify, maintain, and reproduce clinical treatments for anorexia nervosa. The hospital admission and procedures reproduced a regular system of clinical observation and surveillance practices that were presented as being particularly necessary with anorexic patients. The key focus of clinical treatment was the establishment of weight gain. The practice of introducing small amounts of food to patients, that were slowly increased, coupled with bed rest, demonstrate the continuation and maintenance of late nineteenth century clinical practices within the modern hospital previously discussed in Chapter 2.

The severity of weight loss was a key factor in the psychiatrists' decision to transfer the patient to a medical ward or physician. The severity of a patient's weight loss was emphasized through reference to, 'if it were that bad', 'extreme', and 'severe' cases, and this decision also involved ethical and moral aspects for the clinician. The hospital maintained a link between medical and psychiatric discourses through the need to transfer patients for expert management in gastric feeeding programmes. The threat of the patient dying underscored the need to refer to a gastric feeding programme, and like behavioural programmes, the isolation and confinement of patients, and searching of their rooms, presented difficulties and dilemmas to health care workers within the therapeutic relationship.

Anorexic patients become subjects of the practices of surveillance because of the clinical objective of establishing weight gain. These practices, referred to as 'special nursing', involve a nurse's continuous observation of a patient because of her 'unpredictable behaviour'. This practice has similarities with late nineteenth century 'moral attendants' who sat beside the bedside of women patients. The surveillance of anorexic patients is accepted as being necessary because of their need for salvation, whether that need derives from earlier ideas about women's fall from 'moral rectitude', and vulnerability to nervous diseases, or later ideas of women's susceptibility to develop specific psychiatric disorders, such as anorexia nervosa. Anorexic women are characterized by their 'resistance', it is 'one thing in common with all the anorexics', and contrasted with the practitioners' attempts to treat them. This representation of women functions as a clear justification for clinical interventions in which health care workers are positioned as having both the institutional authority and expertise to effect change.

PART III

POSTMODERNISM, THE BODY AND THERAPY: IMPLICATIONS FOR PRACTICE

7
Anorexia Nervosa, Postmodern Readings of the Body and Narrative Therapy

> The human body was entering a machinery of power that explores it, breaks it down, and rearranges it. A 'political anatomy', which was also a 'mechanics of power', was being born; it defined how one may have a hold over others' bodies, not only so that they may do what one wishes, but so that they may operate as one wishes, with the techniques, the speed and the efficiency that one determines. Thus discipline produces subjected and practised bodies, 'docile' bodies.
>
> Michel Foucault, *Discipline and Punish* (1979: 138)

During the early 1980s a more intensive examination of the body, theory and social practices emerged. The body was no longer seen as something that was simply influenced and shaped by external social events, rather it was the object of cultural inscription. The way in which bodies are displayed in social life, their contours sculptured, walk, mix together with others, are sexually available to others, or not, denote cultural discourses about living in certain ways and with particular meaning. In this chapter I discuss theories of the body in which the broader cultural meanings of diet, food choice and body image are highly significant. Sociological and feminist writings about the body, food and anorexia nervosa prefigure in this discussion. Following this I introduce the increasingly diverse theories about food choice and eating, and the significance of the analysis of historical, social, cultural aspects of food to these theories. Further, I illustrate the wider use of social theory to explain food and eating with reference to work in nutrition science and how the examination of social practices intersect with on-going debates in other disciplines. Later in the chapter I critically discuss the extent to which the diversification in theories about food and eating practices and postmodern frameworks of analysis may contribute to a broader conceptualization of anorexia nervosa due to the expanding interrelationships between disciplinary fields.

The use of postmodern analysis to explain the increasing complexities and diversity of social and political life is not new, but postmodernism and the subject of the body is a relatively recent area of developing theory in disciplines such as sociology and psychology. The analysis of the body became a central concern for sociology in the early 1980s. The work of Bryan Turner, *The Body and Society* (1984), and Featherstone, Hepworth and Turner's *The Body: Social Process and Cultural Theory* (1991), provide syntheses of historical examinations of the body drawing on anthropology, sociology and politics, arguing that the body is significant to the study of contemporary Western cultures. Turner's work draws connections between different ontological views of the body and social theories. One of the main developments from these writings is the examination of how the body has become the focal site for contemporary cultural and political practices. As Chris Shilling writes: 'This situation is not inconsequential for the modern individual's sense of self-identity – their sense of self as reflexively understood in terms of their own embodied biography' (1993: 4).

Michel Foucault's writings on the body are a common source of ideas in theories of the body, particularly his notion of how discourse becomes inscribed on 'docile' bodies. Western consumerist culture is saturated with representations of idealized bodies. The discourses that pervade popular culture depict the imagery of vitality, construct specific definitions of body shape for women and men, and produce a plethora of practices that are carried out to achieve embodied perfectionism. For Foucault (1979) these practices are integral to the subjective experience of individuals and in turn reproduce themselves through certain practices. The regular practices that individuals carry out on their bodies become a form of discipline of the body, on a 'docile' body, which is produced by and constitutive of the politics and economics of a society:

> a multiplicity of often minor processes, of different origin and scattered location, which overlap, repeat, or imitate one another, support one another, distinguish themselves from one another according to their domain of application, converge and gradually produce the blueprint of a general method. (Foucault, 1979: 138)

Social and cultural discourses inform and construct a myriad of self-regulatory practices. The construction of individual subjectivity is thus situated within discursive relations and challenges the notion of there being an essential core of individual psychology.

Postmodernism and feminist writings on the body

Social analysis and anorexia nervosa

The analysis of the meanings of food, diet, body shape, body image and weight regulation in Western societies is a significant feature of the examination of the body. These analyses afforded new possibilities for understanding anorexia nervosa in two ways. First, the practices of severe weight loss and its continual monitoring are examined in terms of the way in which social and cultural discourse becomes inscribed on a 'docile' body. Second, the relationship between social practices and subjectivity is explained as being constructed through discourse. Anorexia nervosa is a focus of postmodern analyses of the body because it so clearly illustrates the link between the extreme effects of discourses about women, femininity and thinness within Western culture.

Prior to the new wave of postmodern feminist writings these cultural dimensions of women's experience had already been introduced as being integral to eating disorders. Since the late 1970s feminist writers argued that the social position of women impacts on their experiences of food and the body, and this was previously discussed in detail in Chapter 3. Inequalities in the economic, social and cultural status between women and men reproduce conditions for women to experience low self-esteem and control over individual circumstances. For example, the work of Wooley and Wooley (1982) drew connections between the pervasiveness of the slimming industry and the mounting social pressure for women to be thin. Much of this work centred on the fat/thin issue and the culture of 'slimming'. The politics of weight loss was publicized through several feminist perspectives during this decade that argued 'slimming' fulfilled different functions for women. Lawrence maintains:

> 'Normal' slimming may be due, at least in part, to patriarchal conformity; but anorexia, while encompassing aspects of conformity in its own paradoxical way, is essentially a (self-defeating) striving for autonomy, self-esteem and transcendence of the denigraded female body. (1984: 71)

Further to this, Orbach's (1986) argument that Western societies produced constant dilemmas for women about their identity, and Lawrence's (1984) discussion of the function of food for women to articulate control, became widely known theories. The dominant representations of women as the embodiment of desirable commodities in the media are argued to influence women's behaviour, and that young women in particular take on media images as ideals to strive towards. Instruction for women in how to achieve these images is abundant and a common part of women's magazine culture. Further to this, Rushmer's (1991) analysis of magazine advertisements, describes the representation of women combined with the product itself in physical space, for example, in advertisements for yoghurt and chocolate bars, where the woman is clothed in shiny, chocolate brown, confectionery wrapping. This analysis highlights the cultural connections between women and food that is emphasized by the collapse of women's bodies into the product forms.

Much of this work focused on aspects of a society, as 'influences', which were interpreted as becoming increasingly complex pressures on women that became translated into disordered eating practices. These explanations were significant in drawing attention to the social and cultural aspects of everyday lives, and that these involved gender power relations. Women comprised the main advertising group for food products, particularly for *diet* products as well as *luxury* foods, and women continue to be 'targeted' in advertising campaigns as the key group who is responsible for family eating patterns. The explanation of wider socio-cultural issues in this way did not, however, articulate the interrelationships between culture and subjectivity, except in terms of being *influences* that were separable from individual psychology.

Prior to poststructural analyses in psychology, identity and self were understood using various psychological models/perspectives in which they constituted entities that were separable from social practices. The notion of identity in earlier research was something that responded to external events and/or was influenced by social, political and cultural conditions. Sociocultural analyses of women, food and eating practices, had overwhelmingly explained pressures on women in Western societies as being external to individual women, yet underscored the development of intrapsychic problems. The mother–daughter relationship was particularly highlighted as a problematic site of identity development by a range of medical, psychological and feminist writers. In contrast to this, postmodern theories of the self draw attention to the multiplicity of identities and the ways in which the notions of the self are constructed through social and cultural conditions (cf. Gergen, 1991). Further to this, poststructural interpretations of the social and cultural dimensions of anorexia nervosa do not reify the self as an autonomous entity in the experience of psychological distress.

During the 1980s and early 1990s a proliferation of writings emerged that formulated social theories of the relationship between women, food and subjectivity. The developments in theories of social practices and subjectivity are important to eating disorders, and particularly in the explanation of anorexia nervosa. Language is significant to many of these theories as feminist writers identified the situatedness of women's experiences within cultural discourses about the thin female body. These writers, to various extents, also drew on Foucault's ideas to articulate the cultural production of the definition of femininity. In Western societies the definition and practices of femininity were constructed through the eyes and language of men, constituting what Foucault (1973) termed the 'gaze' of dominant groups.

The interrelations between the body, self and eating disorders became a key focus from the late 1980s and early 1990s. The writings of American feminist Susan Bordo and particularly her work, 'Anorexia nervosa and the crystallization of culture' (1988), are important sources of the reinterpretation of women, body image and eating disorders. This work created a shift in the theorization of women and food. Bordo employed a Foucauldian perspective in a feminist analysis of anorexia nervosa, arguing that it could be understood as the 'crystallization' of Western culture in that it is a symptom of some of the 'multifaceted and heterogenous distress of our age'. Using this perspective, Bordo has re-read socio-cultural images of female bodies and examined 'the political anatomy' of the slender body. Women, she argues, can achieve power through slimming and dieting which she articulated as constituting 'disciplinary practices' for women living within patriarchal society.

Bordo locates anorexia nervosa in specific cultural, political and historical contexts, rather than searching for the causes of anorexia nervosa within individual women. Bordo's concerns reside with the complex and contradictory meanings associated with the cultural representation of 'the slender body' that emerged during the 1980s (Bordo, 1993: 207). She is less concerned with the causes of anorexia nervosa in the traditional sense, and articulates the complexities of various cultural interpretations of individual weight loss. She argues that it is possible to interpret the characteristic revulsion towards hips, stomach and breasts in the woman diagnosed with anorexia nervosa, as an expression of rebellion against maternal, domestic femininity. The contexts that produce anorexia nervosa, for Bordo, are ones that define and instruct women in particular ways of living that accord with dominant males' ideals. This interpretation of femininity is represented in the relative lack of the mothers' power in patriarchal societies. Bordo goes on to suggest another reading in which disidentification with the maternal body may symbolize (as it did in the 1890s and 1920s) freedom from 'a reproductive destiny and a construction of femininity seen as constricting and suffocating' (1993: 209).

This interpretation of women's historical actions may well have been applicable to the middle classes rather than across the spectrum of classes living with very different material conditions. Additionally, within specific historical periods women have become objects and subjects of dominant ideas about sexuality/morality, and evaluated against male norms that also change over time. Bordo is not implying that either reading is the 'correct' interpretation of women's experiences around anorexia nervosa (Hepworth and Griffin, 1995). She is examining the role of anorexia nervosa as a cultural phenomenon at particular historical moments when 'the regulation of desire becomes especially problematic . . . and women and their bodies will pay the greatest symbolic and material toll' (Bordo, 1993: 212).

The translation of the cultural representations of women and body shape into individual psychology involves the development of a range of 'disciplinary practices' on the body, such as weight regulation, definition of body shape contours depicted through the slender ideal, and monitoring food intake to resist fattening foods (Bordo, 1993). Feminist theories, such as Bordo (1993), MacSween (1993) and Robertson (1992), exemplify developments in feminist thinking about the interrelationships between patriarchy, knowledge and power, and the discursive positions of women.

There is a distinction between the work of postmodern feminist writers such as Bordo and her interpretations of the cultural aspects of anorexia nervosa and what I argue here. Writers such as Bordo make important interpretations of why and how the condition anorexia nervosa develops in young women in Western societies related to social and cultural practices of those societies. Rather, I argue throughout this book and elsewhere (with Griffin, 1990, 1995) that the systems of knowledge through which anorexia nervosa is explained within key disciplines are socially constructed. Systems of knowledge construct explanations of the phenomenon of anorexia nervosa in particular ways based on the emergence of specific discourses. The phenomenon of self-starvation is most commonly known today as anorexia nervosa because of the emergence of key concepts that made it possible to construct the definition in the form of a medical discovery over a hundred years ago. Feminist writers who retain the use of anorexia nervosa are also involved in a discursive dilemma in that there is a tension between feminist resistance to psychiatric practice that is oppressive and the continued use of psychiatric terminology, such as anorexia and bulimia, and the individualization of social issues (Hepworth and Griffin, 1995).

Feminist writers have demonstrated the social and cultural dimensions of subjectivity and their relationship to eating disorders generally. These interpretations clearly indicate the continuing diversity of theories about anorexia nervosa and the significance that the analysis of meaning has for developing understandings of popular culture and eating practices across a range of groups. This work has emerged as a continuation of earlier socio-cultural and feminist explanations of anorexia nervosa that I discussed in Chapter 3. In contrast to these writings traditional science areas such as nutrition are also contributing to the diversification of theories about the social meanings of eating practices. In the next section I briefly discuss some recent work that examines social and cultural practices and eating. This work is an example of the evolving interest in the body and social theory within nutrition science.

The diversification of theories about food

Recent interest in the sociology of food has emerged through the work of, for example, (Mennell et al., 1992), government and ethics of nutrition (Coveney, 1996; Coveney, 1998), the history of food (Santich, 1994), gastronomy and multicultural cuisine (Symons, 1993). These authors use various theories to explain the social and cultural meanings of eating and food. These writings have diversified theories about food choice and have significance for the explanation of eating disorders. The analyses, while not specifically addressing anorexia nervosa, examine the breadth and complexities of the socio-cultural dimensions of food choices or the restriction of food intake. While being very different in their theoretical and analytical frameworks such analyses have developed in contrast to what is regarded as a 'modernist' or 'positivist' paradigm of scientific research. Although there is no single form of modernism, modernist theories are depicted by the rationality of arguments, linear relationships and universalizing elements. Recent analyses of food privilege the historical, social and cultural conditions through which the differences between the meanings of food and diet emerge, with some asking postmodern or poststructural questions about the construction and reproduction of food related practices.

Nutrition science and food choice

The broadening interest in food from some environmentalists, sociologists, historians of food and nutritionists, marks a resistance to the standardization of food production, preparation and choice. Sociologists, such as Turner (1982), argue that the modern diet is linked to the broader movement of behaviour regulation that emerged during the seventeenth and eighteenth centuries, particularly in the writings of George Cheyne (1671–1743). During the late nineteenth century the public health movement in Britain provided further momentum to the rationalization of food and eating practices.

Over a century later this rationalization of food has provided a dominant framework for individuals to measure their degrees of relative health and disorder through the narrow focus of the content of dietary intake. The diet regime represents a form of disciplinary practice and government of the body, particularly through modern dietetics, related to the rationalization of everyday life (Turner, 1982) whereby all behaviours are categorized and theorized in relation to dominant ideas about health and disease.

Population health defined in relation to food consumption and diet-related diseases involves the calculation of risk according to most demographic details, including age, sex and socio-economic status, and involving total populations. In the USA, UK and Australia, a series of 'National Goals and Targets' (cf. Nutbeam et al., 1993), identify major morbidity and mortality categories of total populations and their relative risk factors. The key objective for a nation's public health effort is the decrease in morbidity and mortality across a range of disease categories. Public health serves a key function in the regulation of populations in specific ways, termed 'governmentality' by Foucault (1988), that is achieved and maintained through policies, legislation and practices of surveillance. Coveney (1997) expands on the concept of governmentality in research on nutrition education by demonstrating the ways in which discourses about nutrition are used to instruct populations in healthy eating practices. The long-standing tradition of providing information and advice about the composition of healthy eating, weight regulation and disease prevention reproduces the standardization of individual behaviours. One way in which behaviours become reproduced is through the discourse of diet and the popularization of the notion of individual surveillance of body weight.

The nutritional composition of food is a dominant theme in scientific, public health and health promotion discourse about healthy eating. Coveney (1990) has examined nutrition science and public health in Australia and argues for the broader conceptualization of nutrition, including the socio-cultural and gastronomic aspects of food, rather than focusing on purely the metabolic and calorific composition of food. Nutrition science has a traditional focus on metabolic processes in what Crotty (1993) identifies as the *post-swallowing culture* of nutrition research. The more recent focus on the socio-cultural context of food choice and eating she defines as a *pre-swallowing culture* of research.

Gastronomes, historians of food and sociologists have contributed new approaches to food and created a resurgence of interest in eating. They describe a variety of eating practices that existed in the premodern era, through multiculturalism, modernist eras and postmodern cuisine. Knowledge about food and the refinement of one's palate was highly esteemed in Medieval times. The legitimization of pleasure is contained within thirteenth century Arab recipe books that lists six classes of pleasure: food, drink, clothes, sex scent and sound, with food being regarded as the noblest (Santich, 1994).

Symons (1993) traces significant themes in the emergence of the rationalization of food and their explanation in terms of populations, choices and nutritional content. He links these to stages of Australian cuisine and eating. Talking about Australian cuisine Symons writes: 'ours is not even a cuisine in transition, but a cuisine which is post-industrial or postmodern, and up-for-grabs. Ours is a cuisine that demands thinking about' (1993: 10). Symons (1993) locates his discussion of cuisine within a historical context and employs a particular appeal to the notion of 'tradition' and 'traditional ways' to indicate a time when different populations were more connected to the production and preparation of food.

Historical and social analyses of food reintroduce the flavours of food and the pleasures of eating providing possibilities to resist dominant ideas about food-related disease. These possibilities create spaces that move beyond the cultural dimensions of subjectivity that are currently dominated by the centrality of the slender image, diet-based food choice, and the abstinence from foods in the name of self-control, self-loathing or anorexia nervosa. Symons (1993) goes on to make links with reconceptualizing food through rediscovering traditional cuisine where he sees possibilities for the development of discourse on food that incorporates a range of interests about eating; a 'conscious cuisine'. Though, Symons' (1993) analysis of contemporary cuisine defined as a postmodern cuisine is problematic. For example, the excavation of an 'authentic' cuisine to inform contemporary eating practices engenders a notion of authenticity which is subject to criticism in postmodern analysis. Baudrillard writes about the mythos surrounding the location of an authentic origin of cultural objects:

> When the real is no longer what it used to be, nostalgia assumes its full meaning. There is a proliferation of myths of origin and signs of reality; of second-hand truth, objectivity and authenticity. (1983: 12)

Baudrillard (1983) describes the use of the cultural expression of authenticity. Given the indeterminate nature of authenticity it is unclear the extent to which Symons conflates postmodernism with the identification of multiple cuisines and eating practices.

Modernism, postmodernism and theories about food

In the previous sections I have introduced various social theories about the body, feminist analyses of the interrelationships between anorexia nervosa, social practices and subjectivity, and the diversification of theories about food using the example of nutrition science. These readings of the body are useful because they expand the frameworks for understanding anorexia nervosa. Postmodern analysis contributes to this expanding field by examining the ways in which various forms of knowledge produce meanings and practices. As Baudrillard writes: 'Postmodernism is the simultaneity of the destruction of previous values and their reconstruction. It is a restoration in distortion' (1983: 41). The plethora of theories about food preparation, eating and nutrition make key links with social practices. Postmodernism has articulated the theoretical links between the selection, cooking and consumption of food and the inscription of individual identities. In the following sections I elaborate the processes involved in the social construction of meanings about food by discussing postmodernism, discourse and the constructs of 'diet' and 'food', and how these inform discourses about anorexia nervosa. Among the proliferation of information and dietary guidelines that modern nutrition science offers to the public there are few analyses of the social practices that create healthy eating. I argue that postmodern enquiry about key constructs that inform eating practices, such as 'diet' and food', may also inform understandings of anorexia nervosa. None of the analyses that critically examine the effects of dominant scientific discourse interrogate the nature of what is absent in contemporary eating practices. For example, the flavours of food and pleasures of eating are absent from medical scientific, nutrition science and psychiatric discourses about anorexia nervosa. Health care professionals' discourse about food reproduces and maintains a narrow focus on eating explained in relation to scientific indices of nutritional content and weight regulation. This focus is central to medical discourse in the definition of normal and abnormal eating which subsumes the meaning of eating within a dominant framework of pathology. I use the concepts of appearance (Virilio, 1991) and the simulation of meaning (Baudrillard, 1988) to critically discuss the significance of changing subjectivity, the construction of weight loss and anorexia nervosa.

Remembering forgetting: absence in the construction of meaning

The increasing separation of populations from food production and preparation during the late twentieth century is significant to the changing meanings of food. Symons (1993) calls the contemporary dominant food culture a 'car cuisine', because the car has provided the necessary link between people and buying the 'corporate cuisine' of the supermarket. The increasing employment of science and technology to organize eating practices is discussed by Mennell et al. (1992) as resulting in the alienation of individuals from food and what Fischler (1985) calls 'gastro-anomie'.

Previous meanings of food and eating have been displaced by the modern discourses of nutrition, pathology and psychological medicine, that measure the excesses of overeating within the science of obesity, and defines the psychopathology of eating disorders. These discourses isolate the body from the different meanings of food and eating that was once common in premodern times. Talk about the flavours and pleasures of food and eating scarcely exists, or largely constructed through discourses of health and disease. I refer to this talk as absences, or language which has ceased to exist (Hepworth, 1995). Drawing on the work of Virilio (1991), language ceases to exist in the process of the 'aesthetic of disappearance', in that there are moments in our lives when we no longer realize that something is no longer there.

> For these absences, which can be quite numerous – hundreds every day most often pass completely unnoticed by others around – we'll be using the word 'picnolepsy' (from the Greek picnos: frequent). However, for the picnoleptic, nothing really has happened, the missing time never existed. At each crisis, without realizing it, a little of his or her life simply escaped. (Virilio, 1991: 9–10)

The absence of language has implications for the shifts in the meanings of eating because certain discourses eventually cease to be elements in the construction of subjectivity. The shift in meanings of eating articulated through absences involves what Virilio (1991) calls the 'aesthetics of emergence', whereby as certain language becomes absent from use other forms of language use emerge. Just as the flavours and pleasures of eating have fallen from use, the construct of diet has emerged and become a common site for the negotiation of meaning in contemporary discourses about eating. Diet has become a dominant discourse about food, particularly through its relationship with health gains, and the practice of dieting to achieve a socially desirable thin body. The discourse of diet constructs food choice and experiences of eating through these dominant meanings. The problematization of the construct of diet reveals that it is effused with multiple meanings. Diet within a modernist paradigm commonly operates within nutrition science, serves a function in the surveillance of obesity at a population level, and is employed in popular culture as an icon of the feminine ideal. While these discourses about diet are representative of different forms of knowledge, the common focus is on weight control through practices such as calorie counting, weight reduction targets, and the regulation of food choice based on nutrition groups. Through this shift in meaning, the diverse experiences of eating have collapsed into diet-related events that obscure and displace eating and food as pleasure.

*The significance of the image, the constructs of diet and food, and
anorexia nervosa*

One interpretation of how the construct of diet functions in relation to
anorexia nervosa is that diet constructs subjectivity through cultural images.
While the notion of diet has been explained through the historical trajec-
tory of the modernization of the self and regulatory practices of weight
control (Turner, 1982), and body shape (Bordo, 1993), diet is also a construct that is related to cultural forms that change its meaning. The representation of women and food often takes the form of an exaggerated ideal
of the female body. Women are commonly portrayed as succumbing to the
gratification that is found in consuming sweet foods, as consumers of health
foods, calorie counted, low fat and 'Lite' foods. This representation is commonly depicted by a woman's abandonment of self-control as she feeds an
insatiable desire for food, and maintains a link with historical ideas about
women's sexual desire. The image of 'slenderness' acts as a contemporary
metaphor for desire and management of female sexuality (Bordo, 1990).
The historical relationship between women's sexuality and food is associated with the Victorian era when women were depicted, 'in a sensuous sur-
render to rich, exciting food', which was regarded as a form of taboo
(Bordo, 1993). There are similarities between this representation and the
use of women consuming 'luxury' foods, such as chocolate, ice cream and
cake in contemporary advertising. Bordo's (1993) analysis is useful in
emphasizing the centrality of the image in the development of eating disorders, but does not fully explicate the relationships between the image and
eating practices. Drawing on Baudrillard's (1988) writings on the simulation
of meaning through the image and the 'hyperreal' it is possible to further
articulate the relationships between food, diet and imagery:

> hyperreality: that which was previously mentally projected, which was lived as
> a metaphor in the terrestrial habitat is from now on projected, entirely without
> metaphor, into the absolute space of simulation. (1988: 16)

The clarification of some of the complexities of the social and cultural
processes related to anorexia nervosa is achieved by using Baudrillard's
seductive theory of language.

> Seduction is not that which is opposed to production. It is that which seduces
> production – just as absence is not that which is opposed to presence, but that
> which seduces presence. . . . One could conceive of a theory dealing with signs,
> terms, values on the basis of their seductive attraction, and not in terms of
> contrast or calculated opposition. . . . At last, a seductive theory of language.
> (Baudrillard, 1988: 58)

In one sense, food and diets are commonly seen as separable entities in
which food is positioned as, 'tempting', 'irresistible', and invokes a provoca-
tive theme, whereas diets are positioned as 'restraint' and 'control'. Common
to both food and diets are elements of seduction. The dominant meaning that
emerges from either food or diet does not appear in isolation from each
other, as a dualism, but as relational of the theme and challenge of seduction.

Baudrillard's (1988) notion of the seduction of appearances elaborates on the relationships between images and eating by explaining the ways food brings forth and seduces diet, and the way dieting brings forth and seduces the meaning of food. Through this process discourses of diet structure, displace and create shifts in the construction of the self and experiences of food.

There are discourses of food and diet that appear simultaneously, and at times they emerge as being intertwined with one another. The simultaneous appearance and seduction of the language of food and diet displaces the oppositional nature of food and diet. For example, themes of enticement can be found in many food texts. Cakes, ice cream and chocolate have become contemporary icons of media campaigns for 'luxury foods' and described as being 'irresistible', 'indulgent', and 'naughty'. These foods are presented as enticing the consumer, and with which the consumer can entice others, such as the practice of men buying chocolates for women. Women are represented as being in a state of continual struggle with food, to regulate their appetite, sexuality and body weight through the portrayal of luxury foods. This struggle is difficult for some women, and some men. Contemporary eating practices involve regular abstinence from eating certain foods, the construction of eating 'luxury' foods as being 'indulgent', or the perception that one is 'out of control' when large amounts of 'luxury' foods are consumed. For these reasons the simultaneous appearance of food and diet in Western societies involves a process that is as much a struggle with food as it is a struggle with diet.

Feminist analysis has theorized the discursive nature of the image of slenderness in the context of Western society where food is a significant feature of the definition of femininity (Bordo, 1993; MacSween, 1993). None the less, there is no articulation of the multiplicity of meanings of the image and how these make available various subject positions for women. The multiplicity of meanings acknowledges the role of human agency and moves away from positioning women as simply reproducing socially constructed representations of body image. Foucault (1988) conceptualised agency in a postmodern sense as located within and emerging through 'historical rationality', whereby individuals have a capacity to create a reflective distance from social and cultural meanings. This capacity enables the reinterpretation, remaking, or transformation of practices that are more continguous with a 'self', and in turn reproduce, maintain or transform dominant discourses on the body.

Postmodernism and eating practices

The scrutinization of food and eating practices is informed by culturally available discourses about diet and health. The categorization of vegetables, fruit, spring waters and yoghurts are aligned with favourable eating practices, yet often the enjoyment of food is sanitized in the pursuit of health. I have argued that the shifts in meaning about food and diet are explicable through the seduction of language and particularly through the way in which food and diet appear as exaggerated cultural forms. While there is a resurgence of interest in food that presents a range of meanings about food and eating, these interpretations are not necessarily constitutive of a postmodern cuisine or practices. Rather, these interpretations are variants of the multiplicity of modernism. The examination of the interrelations between food and diet, and their simultaneous appearances moves beyond the singular or linear analyses of socio-cultural factors, historical and sociological analyses of food. The emergence of diet as a modernist construct is particularly significant in that it functions to mediate subjectivity in restricting food intake, and the positioning of women as subjects in psychomedical discourse, through anorexia nervosa. Krug, drawing on the writings of Denzin, eloquently describes the complex interrelations that make up the self: 'the intersection of experience and cultural forms is the site where the [postmodern] self is articulated linguistically and formally' (1992: 60). The intersection of experience and cultural forms in the construction of anorexia nervosa involves a particular discursive configuration that reproduces the meaning of restricting food intake by individual women and men. Food has become increasingly understood in relation to images of indulgence, and diet, is the restraint and regulation of eating practices in relation to health and body image. In contrast to the separation of food and diet, the seduction of language explicates the simultaneous appearance of food and diet, the construction of meaning and effects on eating practices.

Social analysis of the body and subjectivity

> Thus the discourse continues, debating whether and to what degree, and in what ways, the body is tomb or temple, loved or hated, personal or state property, machine or self. (Synnott, 1993: 37)

The body is a central area of interest in sociological, feminist, postmodern and poststructural analyses, producing diverse theoretical positions that inform the social and cultural explanation of anorexia nervosa. These analyses locate the meanings of food within theoretical constructions that elaborate and extend the conceptualization of women and subjectivity. Too often though, such theories position women as passive subjects of dominant discourses. Foucault's analysis of the regulatory practices on the body, the 'docile' body, is integral to postmodern readings of the body. In particular, Foucault's later writings on individual subjectivities and the deployment of 'techniques of the self' contribute to a social theory of anorexia nervosa. Postmodernism explains the dynamics of changing social practices, as previously discussed through the writings of Foucault, Virillio and Baudrillard, and affords new ways of understanding anorexia nervosa. However, modern and postmodern theories about the social practices of anorexia nervosa will always be limited if these practices are analysed separately from psychiatric discourse. Social analyses and postmodern theories demonstrate the multiplicity of social and cultural meanings of eating practices, but need to work with and inform medicine and psychiatry. Theories that reinterpret anorexia nervosa must also engage the social and political frameworks that underpin the dominant management practices of anorexia nervosa because these structure the reproduction of practices as well as change.

In the next section I discuss narrative therapy because it is based on postmodern and poststructural analyses in which language is the site for the production of practice. Narrative therapy is an example of a form of psychotherapy that challenges common assumptions about the essential core of the self and psychopathology because language is regarded as both the site of individual problems as well as potential change. 'Personal stories' are privileged within narrative therapy as the focus of communication between client and therapist. These personal stories or narratives are regarded differently across variations of the therapeutic approach, and I only discuss the example of White and Epston's (1989, 1990) work on narrative therapy. Continuing the focus of this book I examine the interpretative complexities involved with narrative therapy and its particular use with anorexia nervosa. This is important in determining the extent to which narrative therapy has the capacity to create possibilities to work with a range of political and institutional dimensions that also comprise the problem of anorexia nervosa.

The promise of narrative therapy

Language, discourse and the social construction of subjectivity

White and Epston (1989, 1990) are most commonly associated with the emergence of narrative therapy and its use as a form of psychotherapy. For poststructuralism, language in all its forms, written, visual and spoken, is the main site to examine and explain social relations and the construction of self. Poststructuralist conceptions of subjectivity developed in contrast to modernist conceptions of causal factors underlying human action. Narrative therapy draws on poststructuralism, Foucauldian philosophy and reinterprets Foucault's writings on discourse. The notion of what constitutes discourse, how discourses operate in relation to social practices and how they come to constitute part of the self, are articulated differently by postmodernist and poststructuralist writers, and was previously discussed in the Introduction and elsewhere. Foucault describes the term discourse: 'discourse is constituted by a group of sequences of signs, in so far as they are statements, that is, in so far as they can be assigned particular modalities of existence' (1974: 107). The meanings of discourse and poststructuralism become increasingly complex through subsequent reinterpretations and through different multi/inter/ disciplinary academic histories.

Simply put, for Foucault (1988) subjectivity emerges through forms of knowledge, power relations and discourses, locating the notion of agency within a conceptualization of *historical rationality*. That is, individuals draw on systems of meaning that are socially and discursively constructed, emerging through historical periods when specific discursive formations come to dominate, and sanction, oppress or marginalize specific social practices. The self is not a discrete and separable entity from social practices. Denzin writes: 'The self which emerges will itself be a tangled web of all that has come before. That is what the postmodern is all about; all that has come before' (1991: 157). Individual meanings and practices are continually changing because the meanings of language are continually in process, as individuals negotiate meanings with others through social interchange.

By making clients' 'accounts', or 'personal stories', central and most significant in the therapeutic process, narrative therapy attempts to understand the *meanings* of distress through client accounts. Narrative therapy while being overwhelmingly associated with the work of Michael White and David Epston, but is not a recent phenomenon. Narrative has a long tradition in various disciplinary fields, such as cultural and communication studies, literary studies, and as a qualitative research methodology, a particular example being ethnography. The intersection of narrative and self in psychotherapy is also understood differently. 'Re-authoring personal stories' involves clients in conceptualizing alternative stories about themselves and others and opportunities to move beyond stories that create distress.

I am not concerned with establishing the 'real' or 'true' interpretation of narrative therapy. Rather, I am concerned with the *general* use of narrative therapy as a phenomenon of the 1990s because it draws on poststructural philosophy and issues that I raise throughout this book. Moreover, anorexia nervosa is discussed as an example of re-authoring personal stories and the narrative therapy approach. Many authors continue to debate the philosophy and ideas underpinning narrative therapy. Gergen and Kaye (1992) reinterpret the singularity of re-authoring and argue there are multiple narratives that construct *narrative selves*. The privileging of clients' accounts is also not confined to narrative therapy. I critically discuss several writings about narrative therapy and examine the assumptions that they make about both narrative therapy as being a unified therapeutic approach, and the internal contradictions of narrative therapy in relation to poststructuralism and Foucauldian analysis.

Narrative therapy and anorexia nervosa

White (1991) writes about a narrative therapy approach to Amy and Robert and how their personal stories relate to social contexts. The story of Amy is one of several discussions of the use of narrative therapy with individuals diagnosed with anorexia nervosa. Amy is a 23-year-old woman who is described as being in a struggle with anorexia nervosa. White (1991) asks the following: how was the anorexia nervosa affecting Amy's attitude towards, and interaction with, herself? What was it requiring her to do to herself? The practices that Amy carries out are commonly seen as being a form of policing her own body. Drawing on Foucault, these practices are termed 'disciplinary practices' that constitute a form of self-surveillance in relation to the norms and dominant discourses of a culture. White continues by engaging Amy in an investigation of how she became recruited into these practices and attitudes.

Externalizing the problem of anorexia nervosa

The most significant aspect of this approach is White's process of *externalizing* the problem of anorexia nervosa through therapy. Externalization of the problem attempts to separate the sense of self of the woman who is bound by dominant social and cultural norms and the woman acting upon her own body in response to those values and norms in terms of the thin ideal by refusing food. This creates the possibilities for a space to exist between anorexia nervosa as a thing that can be acted on and resisted, rather than being understood as an integral part of herself, and the definition of herself through psychopathology.

> In the space established by this separation, persons are free to explore alternative and preferred knowledges of who they might be; alternative and preferred knowledges into which they might enter their lives. (White, 1991: 29)

This method continues to have enormous potential to be further explored as a way of working with women who reduce their food intake. A narrative approach to therapy has the capacity to integrate and work with the range of explanations that women have for reducing their food intakes and does not subsume these accounts into dominant psychological models of human behaviour. However, the extent to which this narrative approach offers the potential for social change through language use is limited. This point is taken up in the concluding sections of Chapter 8 where I critically discuss psychotherapy as an institution within the broader political conditions of health care. I now turn to discuss briefly the philosophical underpinnings of narrative therapy.

Narrative therapy as a genre of psychotherapy

Writings about narrative therapy became so prolific during the early 1990s that it constituted a new paradigm for family therapy. Zimmermann and Dickerson describe the evolution of family therapy and how narrative therapy has:

> led us to think differently about therapy, about clients, and about ourselves as therapists ... we pursue how this different way of thinking has informed a theoretical understanding of a narrative therapy approach and consequently has opened space for different ways of working clinically. (1994: 233)

Zimmermann and Dickerson (1994) trace a brief evolution of family therapy, the advent of narrative and its use in clinical practice. In doing this the authors make four assumptions. First, that White and Epston's (1990)

interpretation and 'application' of Foucault is unproblematic and any critical appraisal is absent. Second, that the selection of particular parts of
Foucault's writings, for use within family therapy, does not involve incon-
sistencies and contradictions within the genre of poststructuralist writings,
for example, that psychology and therapy are constituent elements of discourse, which they do not address. Third, that specific conceptualizations
from Foucault's writings, such as the 'history of the present', became appro-
priated within narrative therapy, and are not as, Zimmermann and Dickerson (1994) write 'borrowed from Michael White (1993)'. Fourth, in that
Foucault's writings have informed the authors to 'think differently about
therapy, about clients, and about ourselves as therapists', these writings are
then assumed to constitute a form of practice that is transferable for use
within clinical practice.

Poststructuralism as therapeutic practice

Accounts that are given in therapy emerge through specific forms of knowledge, discourses, have histories, involve certain incidents, and are described in particular ways with which therapists work. Therapists work with
the language of description of events, of emotion, and of relations that
describe the experience of the world of the client as well as how the client
is constructing an account within the therapeutic context. The interpretation of subjectivity as socially constructed has been taken up with enthusiasm in family therapy. Fish (1993) makes the important distinction between
poststructuralism as therapeutic practice and *poststructuralist informed
therapeutic practice*. This distinction is useful in the delineation of writings
and the discussion of narrative therapy and the use of poststructuralist writings. Narrative therapy (White and Epston, 1990) is represented in numerous texts as constituting poststructuralism *as* therapy. However, the extent
to which narrative therapy can be regarded as poststructuralism as therapeutic practice is contested here.

The interpretation of narrative therapy as a form of poststructuralism in
practice emerged during the early 1990s when writers engaged a discussion
about the philosophical and theoretical premises that narrative therapy
employs. Undoubtedly, conversational and narrative approaches to therapy
are a significant part of family therapy to the extent of being described as
embodying 'a third wave of psychotherapy' (*The Family Therapy Net-
worker*, 1994) and representing a paradigmatic shift for family therapy.
Hoffman is particularly supportive of the move towards narrative therapy
in family therapy, she writes:

> [Family systems theory] now has the chance to profit by another revolution,
> this one in the humanities and human sciences. The postmodern interpretive
> view proposes metaphors for our work that are derived mainly from criticism
> and the language arts. Since therapy is an art of conversation, these metaphors
> are closer to home than the biological and machine metaphors we have been

using. Their particular strength comes from the fact that they are non-objec-tivist and, at the same time, socially and politically sensitive. I am asking you to imagine what a new and different story about 'Family Therapy' might be. (1990: 11)

Hoffman (1990) embraced the formalized introduction of postmodernism into family therapy but did not provide any critical appraisal of the content of changes that were occurring within the field and more importantly ignores the implications these changes may have for the political conditions of therapy as a social institution. In contrast to Hoffman's enthusiasm, Fish writes:

> The narrative/conversational models of White and Epston (1990) and de Shazer (1991) draw only selectively from Foucault and Derrida's ideas, and so perpetuate the constructivist neglect of social context and power. Disregarded aspects of Foucault and Derrida's work do contribute to an understanding of social context and power. Poststructuralism is a dubious prop for constructivist assumptions: its true merit is in its capacity to illuminate the political/cultural context of our practice, including family therapy as a social institution. (1993: 221)

Fish (1993) argues that the various interpretations of Foucault and Derrida's writings are 'selective and flawed'. These writings have to some extent become subsumed within family therapy and at times are distorted to fit this context rather than informing therapy of the social and political nature of therapeutic practice.

Therefore one of the key sites for contestation within this genre of writing is the contiguity between Foucauldian writings and their use as a therapeutic method. Redekop (1995), arguing against Fish (1993), discusses four areas of Foucault's writings in support of White and Epston's (1990) use of Foucault. The first area called 'the relationship of stories and discourse' is most relevant to the interpretative focus of Foucault's work in a therapy context because it has been argued by Redekop (1995) to represent Foucault's interest in personal stories. Redekop (1995) refers to the cases of 'Herculine Barbin, being the recently discovered memoirs of a nine-teenth century hermaphrodite' (HB) (Foucault, 1980b), and 'I, Pierre Riviere, having slaughtered my mother, my sister, and my brother . . . : A case of parricide in the 19th Century' (PR) (Foucault, 1982), as examples of Foucault's interest and in support of the use of poststructuralism as thera-peutic practice.

Redekop's (1995) interpretation of Foucault (1980b, 1982) exemplifies the confusion that exists between the *form* of Foucauldian analysis and the *content* of Foucauldian analysis. Baudrillard's (1988) difference between the *form* and *content* of knowledge explicates the confusion of Redekop's (1995) interpretation of poststructuralist analysis and therapy also con-tributes to Fish's (1993) earlier criticism. The distinction that Fish (1993) makes between poststructuralism as therapeutic practice and poststruc-turalism informed therapeutic practice is crucial to interpreting therapeutic practices. The *form* of poststructuralist enquiry offers an interpretative space to construct alternative readings and meanings of cultural conditions whereas the *content* of poststructuralism can be seen as a series of examples or products emerging through the historical specificity of discursive configurations. The distinction between the form and content of poststructural analysis supports the notion that therapy can be informed by poststructuralism, but that therapy cannot become a poststructuralist practice. Rather, writers such as Redekop collapse content into the forms of practice. Therapy cannot become that which it is already, the object/subject of, through Foucauldian analysis. This argument contributes to the delineation of the conflation between Foucault's (1971, 1973, 1982) analyses that reinterpreted institutional forms of social organization that included psychotherapy, and the appropriation of this analysis within the structural conditions of a client–therapist relationship.

In other words, Foucault does not use (or have an interest in) the case notes and documents relating to HB and PR in the same way as a therapist has an interest in personal stories. This is clarified by interpreting Foucault through the form of his analyses, *interpretative analytics* (Dreyfus and Rabinow, 1982). The form of Foucauldian analysis, interpretative analytics, employs the notion of discourse in a very different way from the notion of narrative. Both discourse and narrative emerged from different, though related, academic backgrounds. Uses of narrative in the genre of literary theory, anthropology and postmodern analyses aim to privilege personal stories, exoticize the domestic and involve issues of representation. Discourse, in the Foucauldian sense, while concerned with the cultural, social, historical and political production of practices, remains less concerned with individual cases except as objects/subjects, not as beginning points of analysis, but as effects. Foucault does not privilege the individual accounts of HB and PR as a therapist would; rather, the uses of HB and PR relate to Foucault's questions and not to questions of therapy that focus on the commonality of change.

Furthermore, Foucault's publications of HB and PR are not examples of the same question. Foucault (1982), while writing about an individual psychiatric case history, namely the case of Pierre Riviere, constructed an analysis of the relations of psychiatric discourses, institutional forms of order, science and truth. Foucault's use of this material, which at this time was genealogical and archaeological form of analysis, was different from the initial construction of Pierre Riviere in psychiatric case notes. Foucault examined the discursive practices through which Pierre Riviere was represented as a case history in relation to the dominance of psychiatric and political discourses:

> Riviere was the accused; the point at issue, therefore, was whether he really was the author of the crime. He was up before an assize court judge which had had the right to grant extenuating circumstances since 1832; what it had to do, therefore, was to form an opinion of him in accordance with what he had done, what he had said, how he had lived, the education he had been given, and so forth. And lastly, he was subjected to a medical examination; here the question

was whether his action and discourse fitted the criteria of a nosographic table. . . . In short, his deed/text was subjected to a threefold question of truth; the truth of fact, truth of opinion, and truth of science. To a discursive act, a discourse in act, profoundly committed to the rules of popular knowledge there was applied a question derived elsewhere and administered by others. (1982: 210)

However, Foucault is not 'applying' poststructuralism to a case history as Redekop (1995) suggests. Foucault examines how Pierre Riviere became interpreted as a madman. The questions for Foucault (1980b) in examining the manuscripts of Herculine Barbin, the nineteenth century hermaphrodite, were different from those of Pierre Riviere. Foucault's (1980b) analysis of HB is situated in a broader context of questions included in his later writings concerned with identity, subjectivity and power. Herculine is examined by Foucault through the analysis of the historical production of 'sex' and the possibilities for a 'non-identity', thus becoming the effect of historical and legislative processes, rather than an example of the discursive construction of a personal story.

Moreover, the notion of *applying* poststructuralism to a therapeutic context, or to any other arena, specifically belies the methodological realm of poststructuralism. An example of this problem is found in the work of Madigan, who claims to map Michael White's 'theoretical and practice orientation ... onto the work of French philosopher historian Michel Foucault' (1992: 265). Social practices, including the therapy arena, emerge through discursive formations, which means that poststructuralist interpretations cannot be 'applied' in the same way as, for example, the systemic approach of the Milan School can be applied to family therapy. Similarly, deconstruction in the Foucauldian sense, while not appearing as an explicit practice in Foucault's writings, create disruptions and discontinuities in knowledges, rather than contributing to unified forms of knowledge, such as the representation of a body of literature and practice which is termed family therapy. Luepnitz (1992), in her reply to Madigan (1992), draws specifically from the comparisons which have taken place between Michel Foucault and Michael White. Luepnitz (1992), like Fish (1993), argues in direct opposition to the appropriation of Foucault's writings within a therapeutic context. Luepnitz writes:

Foucauldian explanation – and post-structural explanation in general – is negative. By this I mean that its project is to criticize and deconstruct – not to advance solutions or new therapies. (1992: 282)

The story of Amy is a discussion of the use of narrative therapy with a person who is diagnosed with anorexia nervosa. Amy and Robert are also examples used by Redekop (1995) in his discussion of White's (1991) interest in personal stories and the analysis of technologies of self and power:

Amy, a young woman with a history of a struggle with anorexia, and Robert, a man with a history of being physically abusive, have stories that parallel those of Herculine and Pierre. (Redekop, 1995: 312)

Let us return for a moment to the interpretation of Amy within a narrative therapy framework. This interpretation illustrates the conflation of personal stories with discourses, and the effects of this on the explanation of narrative therapy. In White's (1991) description he explores the ways anorexia nervosa was affecting Amy's life by employing Foucault's (1988) technologies of the self, yet, only discusses this in terms of individual aspects of how Amy 'compared herself with others', 'policed herself', and became the embodiment of disciplinary practices. While Foucault (1988) examined the local use of power through the notion of technologies, the similarity between narrative therapy and Foucauldian analysis ends there. Narrative therapy reproduces a context for change within the individualizing practices of the client–therapist relationship. During this process the client–therapist relationship may well create alternative meanings through which Amy can reconstruct or re-author her life, but this relationship also displaces the poststructural challenge to individualism, and the possibilities for engaging social structures in change remain absent. To draw parallels between Amy and Herculine ignores the significance of social and historical analysis in Foucault's work.

The form of knowledge that Foucault constructed, including the analysis of *discursive formations*, particularly those through which the domain of psychiatry and clinical practices emerged, the *episteme* and the *relational nature of power*, become regarded as constituent parts of contemporary practices of psychotherapy. The form of analyses that Foucault employed to identify the functions of the dominant discourse of psychiatry and the 'confessional' (Foucault, 1971) become subjugated knowledges through the deployment of these writings as the content of clinical practice in narrative therapy. Narrative therapy (White and Epston, 1990) has been largely interpreted as poststructuralism *as* therapeutic practice. For the reasons I have discussed this interpretation is problematic. Fish writes:

> It is time to ask whether the narrative/conversational approach is being oversold, and too uncritically embraced, particularly in its reliance on limited interpretations of poststructuralism. . . . There is more than one interpretation of poststructural thought, and different understandings have very different consequences for our practice. The interpretations of poststructuralism prevalent in family therapy are, contrary to the expectation raised by Hoffman, (socially and politically sensitive aspects of poststructuralism in family therapy) socially and politically *insensitive*. There are other readings of poststructuralism which have not gained attention in our field and are, in fact, socially and politically sensitive – this poststructuralism which should be informing our practice. (1993: 222)

I have criticized some of the writings that reflect the burgeoning enthusiasm for poststructuralism within family therapy because they reproduce philosophical and theoretical weaknesses in therapy as a social change movement. The representation of narrative therapy as one that employs poststructuralism *as* therapeutic practice and as an unproblematic interpretation of Foucault is particularly criticized. Rather, similar to Fish (1993), I argue that poststructuralism can inform the examination of therapy as a political institution. The political concerns of change in therapy, questions about for whom will the change have benefits, and the location of agency within the discourse–knowledge–power axis, continue to dominate the employment of narrative therapy.

The concerns that I have discussed in the previous sections have less to do with how therapy articulates this axis and more to do with the interpretation of Foucauldian analysis and the construction of narrative therapy within family therapy as a forum for change. In particular, there is no consideration of the extent to which the benefits gained from narrative therapy will endure the complexity of multiple contexts following therapy and sustain the client beyond the first flush of the 're-authored' self. These points inevitably raise questions about the social and political conditions within which narrative therapy is employed and the power relations of changing structures of health care.

The enormous interest in the use of Foucault's writings within narrative therapy is important. Redekop (1995) argues that this interest is a challenge to Michael White's theoretical frame. Rather, I argue that the proliferation of writings are associated with an interest in the interpretations of Foucauldian analysis in order to determine the extent to which post-structuralist ideas can be translated into practices of psychotherapy. I criticize the acceptance that narrative therapy constitutes a form of poststructuralism *as* therapeutic practice. Poststructuralism *as* therapeutic practice subverts Foucauldian analysis by integrating a poststructural philosophical framework into an institutional practice of psychotherapy. In contrast to this Foucault's (1971, 1977, 1980b, 1988) work challenges therapeutic practice as a social and regulatory institution. Therefore, I argue the importance of continuing a debate regarding the interpretative complexities in using poststructuralist inquiry vis-à-vis therapy.

However, in becoming and remaining conscious of the nature of power how much of the debate should be located here? The nature of power must be integral to theory, but it is not always the key question of Foucauldian analysis. In the midst of the appropriation of poststructuralist analysis in family therapy the interpretative complexities involved in drawing on Foucault's writings have been oversimplified. Questions of power have focused on the local position of the therapist, and the use of Foucault's analysis as a therapeutic practice obfuscates the form and content of poststructuralism. The conflation of personal stories with discourses reproduces a limited context for change within the historical individualism of psychotherapy. The use of narrative therapy in relation to the prevention and treatment of anorexia nervosa is discussed further in the next and concluding chapter. The discussion of narrative therapy is extended to the broader social and political context within which psychotherapy functions in the administration of health.

8
Self, Psychology and Participation in the Public Domain

Deconstructive criticism and anorexia nervosa

To summarize, during Part I, I examined the various discourses that have defined and explained self-starvation and anorexia nervosa since around the thirteenth century. I have argued that different ways of thinking about anorexia nervosa and clinical practices develop because knowledge is socially constructed. For anorexia nervosa this means that social practices within certain historical periods give rise to and reproduce particular discourses, or ways of thinking, that make it possible for particular explanations to develop. I have drawn on Foucault's genealogical and archaeological methods of analysis to describe and examine the discourses that construct the category of anorexia nervosa and the effects of this in maintaining and reproducing clinical practices.

The analysis of discourse and practice is significant because it demonstrates that phenomena are not simply the invention, idea or discovery of a historical period; rather, they have emerged through a set of interrelationships between knowledge, social practices and institutional authority. Discourses make sense within, for example, a discipline such as medicine or psychology, and structure the ways in which a problem and/or category of diagnosis, such as anorexia nervosa, continue to be approached. The reproduction of discourses about anorexia nervosa and the maintenance of this category as a psychomedical problem is significantly related to the use of concepts within particular disciplinary fields. The numerous explanations of anorexia nervosa that have developed over the course of the twentieth century is particularly significant, yet treatment outcomes in the long term remain poor. It is my contention that because treatment has remained within the domain of psychological medicine this has reproduced common sets of practices that have limited the extent to which other approaches to anorexia nervosa are seriously considered within mainstream clinical management.

In Part II, I analysed the ways in which health care workers constructed anorexia nervosa and their clinical practices. The health care workers practised in a range of settings, and their accounts demonstrate the ways in which specific discourses of anorexia nervosa are used in practice to make diagnoses, provide reasons for treatment decisions and how food refusal is managed as a form of psychopathology. These constructions provide clear evidence of the structuring of language through historical psychomedical discourse in which women are included as psychiatric patients. Both the health care workers and anorexic patients are the subjects of dominant discourses of anorexia nervosa, and the accounts of uncertainties, dilemmas and ambiguities that practitioners grapple with in practice reflect their attempts to make food refusal consistent with clinical discourse.

In Part III, thus far, I have critically discussed some of the postmodern conceptualizations of the body that theorize subjectivity as being produced through social and cultural practices. Further to this I described the diversification in theories about eating and food in nutrition science that are increasingly focused on social and cultural dimensions. The postmodern turn in the human sciences contributes to the explanation of anorexia nervosa by articulating the interrelationships between language, meanings and social practices. The developing understanding of the body and how bodies are governed locates subjectivity and practices within discursive structures. Poststructuralist and postmodern feminist writings about the body, women's social position and food, explain the onset of anorexia nervosa through the reproduction of cultural discourses. Postmodern analyses challenge the notion of an essential, individual psyche, and theories of causation that exist separately from social practices. Following on from this some of these concepts are employed within psychotherapy; the most well-known being narrative therapy (White and Epston, 1990). This work is critical of traditional psychiatric models of mental illness to varying extents and aims to develop therapeutic practice.

Clearly, theories of anorexia nervosa and therapy have changed, particularly as the functions and effects of language are increasingly articulated and understood. From this understanding there is potential to develop a direction for the prevention and treatment of anorexia nervosa that works with the diversity and complexity of socio-cultural and psychological relationships. In this final chapter I argue for anorexia nervosa to be understood as a public rather than an individual problem, and discuss a more generalized set of theoretical developments which locate a strategic direction within the broader institutional context of public participation in health care.

Deconstructing psychopathology

The practices of medicine, psychiatry and psychology in relation to anorexia nervosa are a major focus throughout the book. I have critically discussed dominant discourses about anorexia nervosa and the effects of psychiatry and psychology in simplifying complex social and cultural practices into a particular form of knowledge and practice about psychopathology. One of the most significant challenges to the psychiatric interpretation of women and anorexia nervosa has developed from feminist analyses. While early feminist perspectives were limited by their use of psychiatric terminology, Susie Orbach, Kim Chernin and Sheila MacLeod, as well as others, maintained a critical voice about the explanation of women and anorexia nervosa. Their criticisms were not primarily directed at psychiatric practice;

rather, they focused on describing women's accounts of the experiences of being in a hostile world. Feminist analyses delineated alternative theories of anorexia nervosa and women, relating the denial of food to an existential crisis, a response to the patriarchal structure of Western societies and psychoanalytic dimensions of women's identity development based on object–relations theory. I have argued in Chapter 3 that these analyses moved the debates about anorexia nervosa away from a conceptualization defined solely by psychopathology towards the recognition of the significance of social and cultural relationships.

I have also discussed social theories of 'self', and how narrative therapy is employed in psychotherapy to create possibilities for women diagnosed with anorexia nervosa to move beyond the language of psychopathology. Within the client–therapist relationship problems are discussed in ways that resist the pathologizing effects of the traditional psychiatric model. The psychiatric model relies on a dominant explanation of anorexia nervosa based on psychopathology that reinforces the dedifferentiation of women from anorexia nervosa. White and Epston's method of externalization positions anorexia nervosa as an object in itself thus creating a distance between the object and the woman. This distance creates the possibilities for the woman to conceptualize the existence of space between anorexia nervosa as an entity that she can act on and resist rather than anorexia nervosa being understood as an integral part of herself, and an identity that is defined by psychopathology. White and Epston's (1990) approach to therapy attempts to reduce the compounding effects of the therapeutic context on psychological distress by examining the practices and assumptions that clients have about specific conditions and the therapeutic process. This method continues to have enormous potential to be explored further as a way of working with women and men who reduce their food intakes. A narrative approach to therapy has the capacity to work with the multiplicity of clients' reasons for food refusal without subsuming these accounts into dominant psychological models of human behaviour.

Additionally, a recent and profound criticism of the concepts of psychopathology has come from within the discipline of psychology in the writings of Parker et al. (1995) who, in *Deconstructing Psychopathology* mount a reflective and forceful attack on psychological and psychiatric practices. With a focus on management practices, the deconstructionist method is argued to open up the places for voices, instead of privileging (medical) reason, for that which reason excludes to be able to speak (Parker et al., 1995). In particular, the authors note, from this critique there are also possibilities for communication through deconstructed discourse. These writings and many others make significant contributions to the theoretical development of complex social phenomena within the health sciences and humanities that address the effects of dominant forms of knowledge.

Given the long-standing criticism of the psychiatric model and increasing theorization of social practices it would be simplistic to assume that there have not been any developments in psychomedical practices. Psychiatry and psychology are not monolithic entities that do not change over time. Furthermore, psychomedical practices are not unified in their application of therapeutic principles. Some mainstream practitioners are aware of feminist concerns and other criticisms of the medical model of anorexia nervosa, the effects of pathologizing women and the limited efficacy of psychiatric treatments. The problem resides in the fact that such critical analyses are commonly regarded in the literature as counter arguments to the dominant medical model, remaining marginalized and having few possibilities for their integration into developing practices. In several countries, particularly the UK, USA and Australia, there is an increasing awareness of the limitations of traditional psychiatric approaches to anorexia nervosa and curiosity to engage with different perspectives. Increasingly the exchange of ideas between traditional medical and non-medical areas is occurring and some psychiatrists have shown scepticism towards traditional approaches to eating disorders. Although, much of this exchange of ideas and collaboration may be largely confined to academic conferences, such as the International Conference on Eating Disorders Conference in London (1997) where feminist and medical approaches are among keynote addresses.

The Social Construction of Anorexia Nervosa contributes to and builds on these debates by describing and analysing the ways in which key forms of knowledge about anorexia nervosa and treatment practices are socially constructed. Moreover, I delineate some of the historical ideas and practices that have constructed the problem of anorexia nervosa in relation to the central concept of psychopathology. So where does this analysis lead to from here? I outline a direction for the prevention and treatment of anorexia nervosa that has the capacity to conceptualize and work across a range of meanings about food refusal. This direction requires a shift away from conceptualizing anorexia nervosa as a psychopathology and towards the understanding of food refusal in relation to social practices. The shift away from conceptualizing anorexia nervosa as an individual problem and towards an understanding of it as a public problem enables a broader consideration of the breadth of cultural, social, political and health care structures. Moreover, the shift in reconceptualizing anorexia nervosa requires a dialogic framework that involves participants in a process of positive change. To elaborate on the conceptualization of anorexia nervosa as a public rather than an individual problem I critically discuss psychotherapy and the need to move beyond positioning individuals diagnosed with anorexia nervosa as psychiatric patients and towards enabling their participation in the public domain as citizens.

Self, psychology and the public domain

Deconstructing psychotherapy

Psychotherapy is organized around particular objectives about treating individual patients/clients, and recent attempts to create more widespread political and social change through the therapeutic arena have limitations. While I do not assume that social change could not result from the client–therapist relationship at a local level, and through resisting positioning individuals within dominant psychiatric discourse, it would be, and has already been found to be, a demanding and lengthy task. To some extent White and Epston's (1990) narrative therapeutic approach is a good example of an attempt to include broader social issues within the client–therapist relationship because social justice is a theme of the therapeutic conversation. However, the structural organization of psychotherapy perpetuates its limitations as a form of empowerment and capacity for social change because the client and therapist work on problems that are the effects of discursive practices rather than the transformation of discourse. For this reason, as well as others discussed in the preceding chapters, it is necessary to shift the dominant conceptualization of individuals diagnosed with anorexia nervosa away from the focus on the clinical management of individual patients towards a position that affords greater possibilities for people to participate in their own health.

The introduction of the notion of individuals participating as citizens in the creation of health care strategies for anorexia nervosa has not been fully explored within the field of eating disorders. It is necessary for this area to be explored before any significant improvement in the efficacy of treatment and prevention strategies can be achieved. By enabling those who are 'at risk' of a diagnosis to participate as citizens within the broader structures of health care introduces possibilities for the construction of a non-pathologized identity through social and political changes.

Approaches to public participation

A common approach to public participation established in Australia, UK and the USA, is organized around the development of policy for specific health problems. Definitions of participation vary, yet a useful differentiation is as follows: 'participation' (negotiated, formalized relationships, shared decison-making, etc.); 'involvement' (citizens treated as individuals rather than organized constituencies, limited decision-making, etc.), and 'consultation' (information sought from citizens on specific plans or projects, little or no structures for on-going engagement between agency sponsors and its publics) (Labonte, 1997).

The frameworks for public participation in health care policy are described in various literatures as *community consultation, community participation, community development* and *empowerment*, and aligned with the New Public Health movement. This movement has developed through an international recognition that health was not merely the absence of disease but required improved social, economic and political conditions. International commitment to health was formalized through conferences and publications, The Declaration of Alma Ata (1978) and The Ottowa Charter for Health Promotion (1986) serving as blueprints for change. Two of the strategies most often evaluated are community development and empowerment that continue to be endorsed in numerous public health policy documents. Historically the significance of community development and empowerment, particularly during its development in the 1970s and 1980s, resides within an emancipatory discourse about specific social groups, or gender, and relationships with health status. Such groups are regarded as being less powerful and lacking control over their lives to improve their health status. As health promoting strategies, the potential of community development and empowerment is sometimes hidden beneath conflicting definitions (Labonte, 1994), political hijacking (Yeo, 1993) and romantic overtones (Petersen, 1994).

The conceptualization of what practices are necessary to effect social changes to prevent anorexia nervosa and improve health status is limited. For example, the notion of empowering a community is enormously complex and difficult to determine. Furthermore, the evaluation of community health outcomes involves methodological biases and diverse contexts that determine the composition of a health outcome. I have argued elsewhere that there are different types of 'outcomes', such as those involving changing social relationships, health development and biomedical status (Hepworth, 1997). The dominant method of working within the empowerment model is for health care or community development workers to work with local communities on short term funded programmes, and this includes its own problems.

In particular these problems relate to the differences in power between experts and the community, and the provision of expert based knowledge and its inconsistency and lack of integration with the knowledge of the participants from a community. Most significantly, the local experiences and knowledge of individuals do not have the potential to create change because such knowledge is interpreted within the dichotomy of 'expert–lay' knowledge about health. Rather, I argue that the kinds of knowledge that particular communities bring to the participation process is constitutive of what Geertz (1983) terms 'local knowledge', in that it is itself a form of expert knowledge. By this I am not arguing for equality between participants to make decisions across all domains of health care, rather that there are equitable and transparent processes of dialogue and decision-making that do not privilege one group over another. Those individuals who participate in decision-making processes are the experts on their experiences and the reasons why change is necessary to improve health.

Public participation and the state

These structures of participation, set up to obtain views from local communities about health-related needs, are very different from a discursive forum where participants are encouraged to engage with a process that addresses general conceptual and structural health care issues. In order to move on from the current limitations of public participation changes are required in these new organizational structures for health. Participation is one form of the much broader state administration of individuals conceptualized in the work of Nikolas Rose (1993, 1994, 1996; Rose and Miller, 1992). Government does not constitute a regulatory machinery that will pervade all areas of social life and administer them for the common good. Rather, liberal political thought is structured around the opposition between the constitutional limits of government and maximizing social and economic processes without the need for direct political interventions (Rose and Miller, 1992). This means that participation within government structures should offer the opportunities for improving health and bear the hallmark of developing principles of equity and social justice issues. For a group of people diagnosed with a psychiatric illness, such as anorexia nervosa, the shift in bureaucratic organization towards participation creates opportunities for them to move beyond the position of patients and become part of a state–citizen relationship.

This structure has many possibilities to work with a range of meanings and issues, and communicate these across various health care sectors. However, these participatory structures, as previously discussed, are subject to enormous criticism. So, why have such structures and communication across sectors resulted in 'tokenism' and continued the marginal position of communities? While these structures allow communities to participate they are also administered domains that emerge at a time when the political administration of individuals allow them to emerge. In such structures the decision-making process invokes a particular form of rationality or reasoning. Therefore, it is necessary to understand the contribution of individuals within the participatory process in relation to the philosophy of state relations.

The conceptualization of modern political rationality, Foucault (1988) argues, was developed during the seventeenth and eighteenth centuries through the general idea of *the reason of the state*. In *Technologies of the Self* Foucault (1988) makes several points about this form of reason, and his third point is most relevant to this concluding chapter because it informs the question 'what is the function of individuals in relation to the state and within the new bureaucratic organization of participation?' Foucault (1988) draws on earlier ideas that appear in Greek philosophy to argue that because the state is its own finality, and since governments have to have permanent reinforcement of the state's strengths, therefore, governments only have to worry about individuals in so far as they can do something for the strength of the state. The individual exists in so far as she or he can introduce change in the strength of the state in either a positive or negative sense. Therefore, it is important to note that structures of consultation are organized around what communities and individuals can continue to provide vis-à-vis the state.

Within this state–citizen relationship there are institutional limits to empowerment and changing health care structures. The notions of self and autonomy, located within this conceptualization of participation, are also defined through an emancipatory discourse that is a particular form of participation that reproduces its own limits. Liberal democracy, as Rose (1993) argues, is bound up with the invention of techniques to constitute the citizens of a democratic polity, which include the definition of and availability of what is considered personal freedoms. Here, Rose (1993) points to a central problem in locating the self within the relations of the administration of health. These relations construct participation as a form of the empowerment of individuals, yet is limited as a process to inform the prevention and treatment of anorexia nervosa.

Taking poststructuralism seriously, the significance of a future direction for making decisions about the prevention and treatment of anorexia nervosa resides with the structure within which those decisions take place, and more precisely the negotiation of language and meaning; a dialogic process (cf. Hepworth and Krug, 1997). This site of negotiation is where there are possibilities for effecting change through the responsiveness of bureaucracies to the multiplicity of public participation and the social contexts in which individuals live. The participatory democratic structure of public participation is a product of government. For this reason it is most important that the structure is developed and maintained in such a way that acknowledges the necessity to understand the diversity of meanings and negotiate outcomes within this structure that are accountable to both government *and* the public.

At present, the process of public participation is neither transparent nor developed. There are no explicit forms of participation, and there are no details about the relationships that different participants, whether they are health care professionals, bureaucrats or public participants, have to effect change. Further to this, public participation processes have not received significant support to explore their effectiveness as a mechanism for local and national changes to improve the health status of those who become diagnosed with anorexia nervosa. The contribution that individuals make to such participation processes requires more serious consideration. For these reasons there is a need for a dialogic process that is explicit. The potential problem for the new structures for participation is that the competing nature of discourse will reproduce discourse itself. One explanation for this reproduction is that the identification and maintenance of specific discourses about an issue or field of research is highly competitive. Particular ways of thinking about anorexia nervosa become reproduced and entrenched within broader systems of disciplinary and professional practices, and are designed to demonstrate that a theory or intervention can provide the answers and solutions. It is, however, the end of an era in which liberal democracies sought truths and answers about particular social problems and the organization of societies (Benhabib, 1992). Conceptual and organizational changes are needed now, and the deconstructionist method takes apart the taken-for-granted assumptions about anorexia nervosa and includes opportunities to transform concepts and practices.

To date the history of anorexia nervosa and women has produced disciplinary divisions, ideological dogma, inadequate multiprofessional collaboration, the separation of expert from lay knowledge and the privileging of psychomedical science. The antagonism between medicine and feminism in the explanation of the causes of anorexia nervosa is a particularly profound example of the tensions that exist in the field of eating disorders as well as other areas of mental health. Throughout the book I have examined numerous explanations of anorexia nervosa, the emergence of these through specific discourses and their effects in limiting possibilities for transforming practice. A key problem in developing the understanding of anorexia nervosa is the competing nature of discourse. For this reason individuals who participate within the new arrangements for the administration of health, from health care fields and communities, need to become reflexive about both the form and content of participatory processes.

No one discourse or discipline can provide the total framework for formulating future directions for the prevention and treatment of anorexia nervosa. A range of knowledge must inform the prevention and response to anorexia nervosa and must always reflect the diversity of all sectors involved. The integration of discourse, ethics, gender, power and justice have to be at the forefront of any negotiation between the state and the changing structures for health care. The recognition of the competing nature of discourse and development of a more reflexive process of public participation is an example of communicative action that aims to reconstruct dialogue to strengthen work between different groups and create spaces for further dialogue.

The postmodern condition has brought with it a set of ways of thinking and structuring human relations that acknowledges and takes seriously the *differences* between social groups and the processes through which multiple voices are heard. Debates will continue about the subject positions and the construction and reconstruction of selves, the conditions for therapy, and the position of health care users as citizens in state relations and participation in a democratic process of health care. What is promising in terms of developing new ways of working with anorexia nervosa is that the discourse of participation relocates the individual subject and self within state–citizen relations. The discourse of participation involves possibilities for changing the language of anorexia nervosa away from psychopathology towards a recognition of social practices and their effects, but for this to occur the participatory process will have to effectively engage a dialogue with the disciplines of psychology and psychiatry. The *psy* disciplines, as Rose (1996) refers to them, but particularly psychology was a form of *intellectual technology*, brought in and out of the public sphere and served the functions of the state administration of individuals and normality. With a more explicit dialogical process in place and carried out by all participants the new arrangements for the administration of individuals will also have consequences for psychology and psychiatry. Just as the spaces for public participation are politically administered, so too will the spaces for psychology and psychiatry be changed through political administration.

The aim of *The Social Construction of Anorexia Nervosa* is to provide an explanation of anorexia nervosa located in terms of discourse and the ways in which social practices are constructed, reproduced or changed. The disciplines of psychology and psychiatry may well be in the last vestiges of reproducing dominant discourses about patients, women and psychopathology, and where these fit within the separation of normality from abnormality. The transformation of practices relies on these disciplines, like the subjects of their dominant discourses, to re-evaluate their roles in the administration of health and participate within the broader explicit politics of the production of knowledge.

References

Acland, T.D. (ed.) (1894) *A Collection of the Published Writings of William Withey Gull: Memoirs and Addresses*. London: The New Sydenham Society.

American Psychiatric Association (1994) *Diagnostic and Statistical Manual of Mental Disorders*. Revised, 4th edn (DSM-R). Washington, DC: APA.

Armstrong, D. (1983) *Political Anatomy of the Body: Medical Knowledge in Britain in the Twentieth Century*. Cambridge: Cambridge University Press.

Astles, H.E. (1882) 'Anorexia in young girls unaccompanied with visceral disease'. Proceedings of the South Australian Branch of the British Medical Association. Adelaide: Frearson and Brother.

Baudrillard, J. (1983) *Simulations*. New York: Semiotext.

Baudrillard, J. (1988) *The Ecstasy of Communication*. New York: Semiotext.

Bell, R.M. (1985) *Holy Anorexia*. Chicago: University of Chicago Press.

Benhabib, S. (1992) *Situating the Self: Gender, Community and Postmodernism in Contemporary Ethics*. Oxford: Polity Press.

Bertagnoli, M.W. and Borchardt, C.M. (1990) 'A review of ECT for children and adolescents', *Journal of the American Academy of Child and Adolescent Psychiatry*, 29 (2): 302–7.

Bordo, S. (1988) 'Anorexia nervosa and the crystallization of culture', in I. Diamond and L. Quinby (eds), *Feminism and Foucault: Reflection on Resistance*. Boston: Northeastern University Press.

Bordo, S. (1990) 'Reading the slender body', in M. Jacobus, E. Fox Keller and S. Shuttleworth (eds), *Body/Politics: Women and the Discourses of Science*. London: Routledge.

Bordo, S. (1993) *Unbearable Weight: Feminism, Western Culture, and the Body*. London: University of California Press.

Bruch, H. (1974) *Eating Disorders: Obesity, Anorexia Nervosa and the Person Within*. London: Routledge and Kegan Paul.

Bruch, H. (1978) *The Golden Cage: The Enigma of Anorexia Nervosa*. London: Open Books.

Brumberg, J.J. (1988) *Fasting Girls: The Emergence of Anorexia Nervosa as a Modern Disease*. London: Harvard University Press.

Burman, E. (1992) 'Identification and power in feminist therapy: a reflexive history of a discourse analysis', *Women's Studies International Forum*, 15 (4): 487–98.

Bury, M.R. (1986) 'Social constructionism and the development of medical sociology', *Sociology of Health and Illness*, 8 (2): 137–69.

Chernin, K. (1986) *The Hungry Self: Daughters and Mothers, Eating and Identity*. Virago Press: London.

Clouston, T.S. (1911) 'The psychological dangers to women in modern social development', in O. Lodge (ed.), *The Position of Women: Actual and Ideal*. London: James Nisbett.

Cohn, N. (1986) 'By love possessed', *The New York Review*, 30 January, 3–4.

Collins, W.J. (1894) 'Anorexia nervosa', *The Lancet*, 27 January, 202–3.

Cousins, M. and Hussain, A. (1984) *Michel Foucault*. New York: St. Martin's Press.

Coveney, J. (1990) 'Towards 2000 – Planning the dietetic odyssey'. *Dietitians Association of Australia National Conference Proceedings*, No. 9, 33–6.

Coveney, J. (1996) 'The Government and Ethics of Nutrition'. Unpublished PhD Thesis, Murdoch University, Australia.

Coveney, J. (1998) 'The government and ethics of health promotion: the importance of Michel Foucault', *Health Education Research*.

Crisp, A.H. (1980) *Anorexia Nervosa: Let Me Be*. London: Academic Press.

Crotty, P. (1993) 'The value of qualitative research in nutrition', *Annual Review of Health Social Sciences*, 3: 109–18.

Dally, P. and Gomez, J. (1979) *Anorexia Nervosa*. London: Heinemann.

Davis, K. (1988) *Power Under the Microscope*. Netherlands: Foris.

Denzin, N. K. (1991) *Images of Postmodern Society*. London: Sage.

de Shazer, S. (1991) *Putting Difference to Work*. New York: W.W. Norton.

Dreyfus, H.L. and Rabinow, P. (1982) *Michel Foucault. Beyond Structuralism and Hermeneutics*. 2nd edn. Chicago: University of Chicago Press.

Ehrenreich, B. and English, D. (1978) 'The "sick" women of the upper classes', in J. Ehrenreich (ed.), *The Cultural Crisis of Modern Medicine*. New York: Monthly Review Press.

Ehrenreich, B. and English, D. (1979) *For Her Own Good: 150 Years of Experts' Advice to Women*. London: Pluto Press.

Featherstone, M., Hepworth, M. and Turner, B. (1991) *The Body: Social Processes and Cultural Theory*. London: Sage.

Fee, E. (1981) 'Is feminism a threat to scientific objectivity?', *International Journal of Women's Studies*, 4: 378–92.

Ferguson, J.M. (1993) 'The use of electroconvulsive therapy in patients with intractable anorexia nervosa', *International Journal of Eating Disorders*, 13 (2): 195–201.

Fischler, C. (1979) 'Gastro-nomie et gastro-anomie: sagesse du corps et crises bioculturelle de l'alimentation?' *Communications*, 31: 189–210.

Fish, V. (1993) 'Poststructuralism in family therapy: interrogating the narrative/conversational mode', *Journal of Marital and Family Therapy*, 19 (3): 221–32.

Fisher, S. and Todd, A.D. (eds) (1983) *The Social Organisation of Doctor–Patient Communication*. Washington, DC: Centre for Applied Linguistics.

Foucault, M. (1971) *Madness and Civilisation: A History of Insanity in the Age of Reason*. London: Tavistock Press.

Foucault, M. (1973) *The Birth of the Clinic: An Archaeology of Medical Perception*. London: Tavistock Press.

Foucault, M. (1974) *The Archaeology of Knowledge*. London: Tavistock Press.

Foucault, M. (ed.) (1982) *I, Pierre Rivière, having slaughtered my mother, my sister, and brother . . . : A case of parricide in the 19th century*. London: University of Nebraska Press.

Foucault, M. (1977) *Discipline and Punish: The Birth of the Prison*. New York: Vintage Books.

Foucault, M. (1980a) *The History of Sexuality*. Vol. 1: An Introduction. New York: Vintage Books.

Foucault, M. (ed.) (1980b) *Herculine Barbin, Being the Recently Discovered Memoirs of a Nineteenth Century Hermaphrodite*. Trans. Richard McDongall. New York: Colophon.

Foucault, M. (1988) 'The political technology of individuals', in L.H. Martin, H. Gutman, and P.H. Hutton (eds), *Technologies of the Self: A Seminar with Michel Foucault*. Amherst: University of Massachusetts Press.

Freud, S. (1973 [1933]) *New Introductory Lectures on Psychoanalysis*, in A. Richards (ed.), Freud Pelican Library, Vol. 2. Harmondsworth: Penguin.

Gardner, L.I. (1972) 'Deprivation dwarfism', *Scientific American*, July, 101–7.

Garfinkel, P.E. and Garner, D.M. (1982) *Anorexia Nervosa: A Multidimensional Perspective*. New York: Bruner Mazel.

Garner, D.M., Olmstead, M.P. and Polivy, J. (1983) 'The development and validation of a multidimensional eating disorder inventory for anorexia nervosa and bulimia', *International Journal of Eating Disorders*, 2: 15–34.

Geertz, C. (1983) *Local Knowledge: Further Essays in Interpretive Anthropology*. New York: Basic Books.

Gergen, K.J. (1985) 'The social constructionist movement in modern psychology', *American Psychologist*, 40: 266–75.

Gergen, K.J. (1991) *The Saturated Self: Dilemmas of Identity in Contemporary Life*. New York: Basic Books.

Gergen, K. and Kaye, J.D. (1992) 'Beyond narrative in the negotiation of therapeutic meaning', in S. McNamee and K. Gergen (eds), *Therapy as Social Construction*. London: Sage.

Gilbert, G.N. and Mulkay, M. (1984) *Opening Pandora's Box: A Sociological Analysis of Scientists' Discourse*. Cambridge: Cambridge University Press.

Goffman, E. (1968) *Asylums*. London: Penguin.

Griffin, C. (1982) 'The Good, the Bad and the Ugly: Images of Young Women in the Labour Market'. Stencilled occasional paper, Centre for Contemporary Cultural Studies, University of Birmingham.

Gull, W.W. (1868) 'The Address in Medicine: delivered before the annual meeting of the B.M.A. at Oxford', *The Lancet*, 8 August.

Gull, W.W. (1874) 'Anorexia Nervosa (Apepsia Hysterica, Anorexia Hysterica)', *Transactions of the Clinical Society*. London, 7, 22–7.

Gull, W.W. (1888) 'Anorexia Nervosa', *The Lancet*, 17 March, 516–17.

Harper, D.J. (1994) 'Histories of suspicion in a time of conspiracy: a reflection on Aubrey Lewis's history of paranoia', *History of the Human Sciences*, 7 (3): 89–109.

Hasted, R. (1984) 'The new myth of the witch', *Trouble and Strife*, 2, Spring.

Hawkings, J.R., Jones, K.S., Sim, M. and Tibbets, R.W. (1956) 'Deliberate disability', *British Medical Journal*, 18 February, 361–7.

Henriques, J.W., Hollway, C., Urwin, C., Venn, C. and Walkerdine, V. (1984) *Changing the Subject: Psychology, Social Regulation and Subjectivity*. London: Methuen.

Hepworth, J. (1991) *A Post-Structuralist Analysis of the Late 19th Century Medical Discovery of Anorexia Nervosa and Contemporary Discourses on Anorexia Nervosa Used by Health Care Workers*. Unpublished PhD Thesis, University of Birmingham, UK.

Hepworth, J. (1994) 'Qualitative analysis and eating disorders: discourse analytic research on anorexia nervosa', *International Journal of Eating Disorders*, 15 (2): 179–85.

Hepworth, J. (1995) 'The seduction of diet'. Conference Proceedings Framing Communication: Exclusions, Edges and Cores. *Australian and New Zealand Communication Association National Conference*, 5–7 July, Perth.

Hepworth, J. (1997) 'Evaluation in health outcomes research: linking theories, methodologies and practice in health promotion', *Health Promotion International,* 12 (3): 233–8.

Hepworth, J. and Griffin, C. (1990) 'The discovery of anorexia nervosa: discourses of the late 19th Century'. *Text*, 10 (4): 321–38.

Hepworth, J. and Griffin, C. (1995) 'Conflicting opinions? "Anorexia nervosa", medicine, and feminism', in, S. Wilkinson and C. Kitzinger (eds), *Feminism and Discourse.* London: Sage.

Hepworth, J. and Krug, G.J. (1997) 'Hepatitis C and policy implementation: ethics as a dialogic process', *Australian and New Zealand Journal of Public Health,* 21(1): 4–7.

Hoffman, L. (1990) 'Constructing realities: an art of lenses', *Family Process*, 29: 1–12.

Hollway, W. (1989) *Subjectivity and Method in Psychology*. London: Sage.

Horsfall, J. (1991) 'The silent participant: Bryan Turner on anorexia nervosa', *Australian and New Zealand Journal of Sociology*, 27 (2): 232–4.

Jordanova, L. (1995) 'The social construction of medical knowledge', *Social History of Medicine*, 8 (3): 361–81.

Kennedy, E. and Mendus, S. (eds) (1989) *Women in Western Political Philosophy*. London: Wheatsheaf.

Klein, M. (1959) *The Psychoanalysis of Children*. Revised ed. London: Hogarth Press.

Krug, G. (1992) 'Visual ethnographies and the postmodern self: reflections on aesthetics and metatext', in N.K. Denzin (ed.), *Studies in Symbolic Interaction: A Research Annual*. London: JAI Press Inc.

Labonte, R. (1994) 'Health promotion and empowerment: reflections and professional practice', *Health Education Quarterly*, 21 (2): 253–68.

Labonte, R. (1997) 'Participation in health promotion: the "hardware" and the "software"', in R. Labonte (ed.), *Power, Participation and Partnerships for Health Promotion*. Victorian Health Promotion Foundation, Australia.

Laing, R.D. and Esterson, A. (1964) *Sanity, Madness and the Family*. London: Penguin.

Laseque, E.C. (1873) 'On Hysterical Anorexia', *Medical Times and Gazette*, 6 September: 265–6; 27 September: 367–9.

Lawrence, M. (ed.) (1984) *The Anorexic Experience*. London: The Women's Press.

Lawrence, M. (ed.) (1987) *Fed Up and Hungry*. London: The Women's Press.

Lawrence, M. and Lowenstein, C. (1979) 'Self-starvation', *Spare Rib*, No. 83.

Leon, G.R. (1980) 'Is it bad not to be thin?', *American Journal of Clinical Nutrition*, 33: 174–6.

Leupnitz, D. (1992) 'Nothing in common but their first names: the case of Foucault and White', *Journal of Family Therapy*, 14 (3): 281–4.

Lloyd, J.H. (1893) 'Hysterical tremor and hysterical anorexia (anorexia nervosa) of a severe type'. *The American Journal of Medical Science* 106: 264–277.

Lyons, A.S. and Petrucelli, R.J. (ii) (1978) *Medicine: An Illustrated History.* New York: Harry N. Abrams.

MacLeod, M. and Saraga, E. (1988) 'Challenging the orthodoxy: towards a feminist theory and practice', *Feminist Review*, Spring, 28: 16–55.

MacLeod, S. (1981) *The Art of Starvation*. London: Virago.

MacSween, M. (1993) *Anorexic Bodies: A Feminist and Sociological Perspective on Anorexia Nervosa*. London: Routledge.

Madigan, S. (1992) 'The application of Michel Foucault's philosophy in the problem external-izing discourse of Michael White', *Journal of Family Therapy*, 14 (3), 1265–279.

Marchant, H. and Smith, H. (1977) *Adolescent Girls at Risk*. London: Pergamon Press.

Marshall, C.F. (1895) 'A fatal case of anorexia nervosa', *The Lancet*, 19 January, 149–50.

Masson, J.M. (1985) *The Assault on Truth*. London: Penguin.

Mennell, S., Murcott, A. and Otterloo (1992) *The Sociology of Food: Eating, Diet and Culture*. London: Sage.

Minuchin, S., Rosman, B.L. and Baker, L. (1978) *Psychosomatic Families: Anorexia Nervosa in Context*. Cambridge, MA: Harvard University Press.

Mitchell, J. (1975) *Psychoanalysis and Feminism*. London: Penguin.

Morgan, H.G. (1977) 'Fasting girls and our attitudes to them', *British Medical Journal*, 2: 1652–55.

Morton, R. (1694) *Phthisiologia: or a Treatise of Consumptions*. London: Smith and Walford.

Mulkay, M., Potter, J. and Yearly, S. (1982) 'Why an analysis of scientific discourse is needed', in K.D. Knorr-Cetina and M. Mulkay (eds), *Science Observed: Perspectives on the Social Study of Science*. Beverly Hills, CA: Sage.

Nemiah, J.C. (1958) 'Anorexia nervosa: facts and theory, *American Journal of Digestive Dis-eases*, 3 (4): 249–74.

Nicolson, M. and McLaughlin, C. (1987) 'Social constructionism and medical sociology: a reply to M.R. Bury', *Sociology of Health and Illness*, 9 (2): 107–26.

Nutbeam, D., Wise, M., Bauman, A., Harris, E. and Leeder, S. (1993) *Goals and Targets for Australia's Health in the Year 2000 and Beyond*. Canberra: Australian Government Publish-ing Service.

Orbach, S. (1978) *Fat is a Feminist Issue*. London: Hamlyn.

Orbach, S. (1986) *Hunger Strike: The Anorectic's Struggle as a Metaphor for Our Age*. London: Faber and Faber.

Palmer, R.L. (1980) *Anorexia Nervosa*. London: Penguin.

Parker, I. (1989) *The Crisis in Modern Social Psychology – and How to End It*. London: Routledge.

Parker, I. (1992) *Discourse Dynamics: Critical Analysis for Social and Individual Psychology*. London: Routledge.

Parker, I., Georgaca, E., Harper, D., McLaughlin, T. and Stowell-Smith, M. (1995) *Decon-structing Psychopathology*. London: Sage.

Parrinder, G. (1958) *Witchcraft*. London: Penguin.

Petersen, A. (1994) 'Community development in health promotion: empowerment or regu-lation?', *Australian Journal of Public Health*, 18 (2): 213–17.

Potter, J. and Wetherell, M. (1987) *Discourse and Social Psychology: Beyond Attitudes and Behaviour*. London: Sage.

Redekop, F. (1995) 'The "problem" of Michael White and Michel Foucault', *Journal of Marital and Family Therapy*, 21 (3): 309–18.

Robertson, M. (1992) *Starving in the Silences*. Sydney: Allen and Unwin.

Rose, N. (1993) 'Towards a Critical Sociology of Freedom'. Inaugural lecture delivered on 5 May 1992, Goldsmiths College, University of London. Goldsmiths College Occasional Paper.

Rose, N. (1994) 'Government, authority and expertise under advanced liberalism', *Economy and Society*, 22 (3): 273–99.

Rose, N. (1996) *Inventing Our Selves: Psychology, Power and Personhood*. Cambridge: Cambridge University Press.

Rose, N. and Miller, P. (1992) 'Political power beyond the state: problematics of government', *British Journal of Sociology*, 43 (2): 172–205.

Rushmer, R. (1991) 'How advertisers portray women in the "glossies"'. Research presented at the Women and Psychology Conference, July.

Ryle, J.A. (1936) 'Anorexia nervosa', *The Lancet*, 17 October, 893–9.

Santich, B. (1994) *The Original Mediterranean Cuisine*. Adelaide: Wakefield Press.

Sayers, J. (1982) *Biological Politics: Feminist and Anti-Feminist Perspectives*. London: Tavistock.

Sayers, J. (1986) *Sexual Contradictions: Psychology, Psychoanalysis and Feminism*. London: Tavistock.

Scull, A.T. (1982) *Museums of Madness*. London: Penguin.

Scull, A. (1993) *The Most Solitary of Afflictions: Madness and Society in Britain 1700–1900*. London: Yale University Press.

Seidman, S. and Wagner, D. (eds) (1991) *Postmodernism and Social Theory*. New York: Basil Blackwell.

Selvini-Palazzoli, M. (1974) *Self-Starvation: From the Intrapsychic to the Transpersonal Approach to Anorexia Nervosa*. London: Human Context Books.

Shilling, C. (1993) *The Body and Social Theory*. London: Sage.

Shotter, J. and Gergen, K.J. (1989) *Texts of Identity*. London: Sage.

Showalter, E. (1987) *The Female Malady: Women, Madness and English Culture 1830–1980*. London: Virago.

Simmonds, M. (1914) Ueber embolische Prozesse in der Hypophysis, *Virchows Archiv (Pathologische Anatomie)*, 217: 226–39.

Smart, B. (1983) *Foucault, Marxism and Critique*. London: Routledge and Kegan Paul.

Stephens, L. (1895) 'Emsworth cottage hospital, case of anorexia nervosa; necropsy', *The Lancet*, 5 January, 31–2.

Sturrock, J. (1986) *Structuralism*. London: Paladin.

Suleiman, S.R. (1986) *The Female Body in Western Culture: Contemporary Perspectives*. Cambridge, MA: Harvard University Press.

Symons, M. (1993) *The Shared Table: Ideas for an Australian Cuisine*. Canberra: Australian Government Publishing Service.

Synnott, A. (1993) *The Body Social: Symbolism, Self and Society*. London: Routledge.

Szasz, T. (1971) *Manufacture of Madness*. London: Routledge and Kegan Paul.

Szasz, T. (1972) *The Myth of Mental Illness*. London: Paladin.

Turner, B. (1982) 'The government of the body, medical regimens, and the rationalisation of diet', *British Journal of Sociology*, 33 (2): 252–69.

Turner, B. (1984) *The Body and Society, Explorations in Social Theory*. Oxford: Basil Blackwell.

Turner, B.S. (1987) *Medical Power and Social Knowledge*. London: Sage.

Turner, B. (1990) 'The talking disease: Hilde Bruch and anorexia nervosa', *Australian and New Zealand Journal of Sociology*, 26 (2): 157–69.

Ussher, J. (1991) *Women's Madness: Misogyny or Mental Illness?* Hemel Hempstead: Harvester Wheatsheaf.

Vandereycken, W. and Beumont, P.J.V. (1990) 'The first Australian case description of anorexia nervosa', *Australian and New Zealand Journal of Psychiatry*, 24: 109–12.

Vandereycken, W. and Lowenkopf, E.L. (1990) 'Anorexia nervosa in 19th century America', *The Journal of Nervous and Mental Disease*, 178: 531–5.

Vandereycken, W., Kog, E. and Vanderlinden, J. (1989) *The Family Approach to Eating Disorders: Assessment and Treatment of Anorexia Nervosa and Bulimia*. New York: PMA Publications.

Virilio, P. (1991) *The Aesthetics of Disappearance*. New York: Semiotext.

Walker Bynum, C. (1991) *Fragmentation and Redemption: Essays on Gender and the Human Body in Medieval Religion*. New York: Urzone, Inc. Zone Books.

White, M. (1991) 'Deconstruction and therapy'. *Dulwich Centre Newsletter,* No. 3.

White, M. and Epston, D. (1989) *Literate Means to Therapeutic Ends.* Adelaide: Dulwich Centre Publications.

White, M. and Epston, D. (1990) *Narrative Means to Therapeutic Ends.* New York: W.W. Norton.

White, M. (1993) 'Deconstruction and Therapy'. In S. Gilligan and R. Price (eds) *Therapeutic Conversations* (pp. 22–61). New York: W.W. Norton,

Winnicott, D.W. (1964) *The Child, The Family and the Outside World*. London: Penguin.

Wooley, O.W. and Wooley, S.C. (1982) 'The Beverley Hills eating disorder: the mass marketing of anorexia nervosa', *International Journal of Eating Disorders,* 1 (3): 57–69.

World Health Organisation (1986) 'Health promotion: Ottowa Charter for Health Promotion', *Health Promotion,* 1 (4): 1–5.

World Health Organisation/UNICEF (1978) 'Alma Ata 1978 Primary Health Care Health Care For All Series 1'. Geneva: WHO.

Yeo, M. (1993) 'Toward an ethic of empowerment for health promotion', *Health Promotion International,* 8 (3): 225–35.

Zimmermann, J.L. and Dickerson, V.C. (1994) 'Using a narrative metaphor: implications for theory and clinical practice', *Family Process,* 33: 233–45.

INDEX